GOD SAW THAT IT WAS GOOD

A Safari THROUGH Salvation History

BRANT LAW

PARACLETE PRESS
BREWSTER, MASSACHUSETTS

2021 First Printing

God Saw That It Was Good: A Safari through Salvation History

Text copyright © 2021 by Brant Law

ISBN 978-1-64060-492-6

  Library of Congress Cataloging-in-Publication Data
Names: Law, Brant, 1981- author.
Title: God saw that it was good : a safari through salvation history /
  Brant Law.
Description: Brewster, Massachusetts : Paraclete Press, 2021. | Includes
  bibliographical references. | Summary: "Some of the amazing animal
  stories in the Bible used to help us appreciate how God sometimes uses
  animals to draw us closer to him and to guide us in the life he wants us
  to live"-- Provided by publisher.
Identifiers: LCCN 2020044725 (print) | LCCN 2020044726 (ebook) | ISBN
  9781640604926 | ISBN 9781640604933 (mobi) | ISBN 9781640604940 (epub) |
  ISBN 9781640604957 (pdf)
Subjects: LCSH: Animals in the Bible. | Animals--Religious
  aspects--Christianity. | Bible stories.
Classification: LCC BS663 .L39 2021 (print) | LCC BS663 (ebook) | DDC
  220.8/59--dc23
LC record available at https://lccn.loc.gov/2020044725
LC ebook record available at https://lccn.loc.gov/2020044726

10 9 8 7 6 5 4 3 2 1

Published by Paraclete Press
Brewster, Massachusetts
www.paracletepress.com

Printed in the United States of America

contents

INTRODUCTION

My in-laws hate animals. They are the sweetest, kindest, most loving people that I have ever had the pleasure of meeting, but that love does not extend into the realm of the animal kingdom. My wife inevitably imbibed some of their perspective. So, during our marriage preparation class, the only serious concern our priest had for our impending matrimony was that I loved animals and she did not. He asked, "Is having pets a problem that both of you can work through lovingly and in an amicable way?" We confidently agreed, yes.

Then one evening, a year or so after we were married, my mom called and asked us to babysit a kitten over the weekend while she went out of town. We agreed, and Bella came over to stay at our home and has never left.

What happened that night that caused this change in my wife's heart? As we lay in bed, sleeping soundly, we were both awakened by a soft mewing sound at the foot of our bed. We glanced down and found Bella, snaking her way through a maze of jumbled blankets to lay her tiny body between us and rest by our side. As she slept peacefully, her soft purrs and cat snores could be heard, and they melted away my wife's animal-hardened heart.

Now, almost three years and two indoor cats later, my wife has been won over to the animal kingdom. She asked me the other evening if I knew how much she loved Bella. I replied, no. She then told me that her love for Bella was limitless.

She may have been exaggerating slightly, but what she said shows how animals can actually help us glimpse the divine. In this instance, because of a cat, my wife was able to gain a tangible understanding of what it means to love through the depths and heights of infinity—the love that only describes the Father, Son, and Holy Spirit.

I hope this book brings you the same gift my wife experienced, a glimpse of God through his creation on the backs, whiskers, scales, and wings of our furry and sometimes not so furry friends. This is not a book of biblical commentary on passages of Scripture, theological reflections, or a book about the lives of the saints, though there are some of these things in each chapter. This book is a collection of some of the more famous and not so famous stories about animals in the Bible, the lives of saints, and sometimes from my own life, presented to you to not only learn of these amazing tales about animals, but to also appreciate how God uses his creation to draw us closer to him and guide us to the life he wants us to live.

As the *Catechism of the Catholic Church* says in paragraph #2415, "Animals, like plants and inanimate beings, are by nature destined for the common good of past, present, and future humanity," and in paragraph #2416, "Animals are God's creatures. He surrounds them with his providential care. By their mere existence they bless him and give him glory." I hope this book can in some way illuminate these teachings and kindle in our hearts a love and appreciation for all God's creatures.

Perhaps you have lost some of the wonder and joy of life somewhere along the way. God and his beauty are always surrounding us in the most intriguing and fun ways. It is my aim that some of these quirky stories and thoughts will bring a smile to your face and help to reopen the eyes of faith in your heart.

THE NOBLE DONKEY

" Samson used a jawbone of an ass
to slay a thousand Philistines.
Imagine what you can do with an entire ass."
—St. John Vianney

'm a high school math teacher. This is a position I have loved and tried to carry out to the best of my ability for the past fifteen years. However, since becoming married, I unknowingly acquired another, sort of unofficial, job and title at work, that of cheer donkey.

You might be asking, what on earth is a cheer donkey? My wife is a national champion cheerleading coach at the high school in Arkansas where we both work. When I married her, I also married into the sport of cheerleading. I found myself attending practices and competitions, not because I know anything at all about competitive cheerleading, but because I discovered I am really good at carrying things for my wife and the girls on the team. I can carry pom poms, megaphones, lipstick, hair spray, bows, signs, audio equipment, backpacks, and other cheerleading essentials to and from these practices and competitions. Over the years, instead of a pack mule, I have been lovingly named by the girls, the cheer donkey.

That's fine with me. I'm not at all unhappy about being named after a donkey. In fact, I think it's a shame that such a noble creature, with so many amazing stories in Scripture and the lives of saints, is now associated with a curse word.

One thing I have learned about being a cheer donkey for a high school cheerleading team is that it is never about the cheer donkey. It is always about the girls and my wife. I do whatever I can to try and make their performances easier and less stressful by keeping my head down and my mouth shut, while moving their equipment wherever they may need me to move it. I simply try to serve, not be served. It is not about me. This is one of the great virtues that real donkeys throughout salvation history have taught us about our spiritual lives.

Donkeys in the Bible

Sacred Scripture utilizes the donkey as a symbol of humility because it is truly an animal for the poor that brings down those perceived to be mighty.[1] In several instances in the Old and New Testaments, a donkey also points our gaze toward God's power and the coming of the long-awaited Messiah.

Granted, our first instance is a bit gruesome.

In the Book of Judges 15:15–17, Samson picks up the jawbone of an ass (aka, a donkey) and uses it to slay one thousand Philistines in battle. In this story, Samson's wife is murdered by the Philistines and he vows to take revenge against them. Samson is then captured and brought to the Philistine camp, when the "Spirit of the Lord" comes upon him and gives him the strength to break his bonds. Free of confinement, he finds the jawbone of an ass lying on the ground. Grasping it in his hand, he fights off and slays one thousand of his captors. After the battle, Samson tosses his blood-soaked weapon into the air in victory, forever naming the field of battle as *Ramath-lehi*, which in Hebrew means "Jawbone Hill."

Theologian John A. Grindel, CM, says, "When Samson sees the Philistines the spirit of the Lord comes upon him, moving him once again to extraordinary action."[2] This "extraordinary action" is not only God's power over his creation, but also the power of a humble faith in God. A donkey's jawbone is only about nine inches in length.[3] The proud Philistines, attacking Samson on all sides with swords much stronger and longer than a simple jawbone, must have been supremely confident rushing at Samson to strike him down. How the mighty were humbled on the battlefield that day by the simple, long-discarded remains of an animal used by the poor of Israel for their everyday needs. God truly humbles those who consider themselves mighty and raises up the lowly.

Another example of a donkey being used as a symbol of humility in Scripture is located in the Old Testament book of Zechariah. In this account, the humble donkey is one of the signs used in prophecy to identify the coming of the King of Israel. Zechariah 9:9 says, "Exult greatly, O daughter Zion! Shout for joy, O daughter Jerusalem! Behold: your king is coming to you, a just savior is he, Humble, and riding on a donkey, on a colt, the foal of a donkey."

This statement was probably laughed at by many in Israel as they awaited a messiah to come and conquer their foes. A king riding atop a long-eared, buck-toothed, pot-bellied donkey hardly fits the description of a mighty king who will restore the temple and the kingdom of Israel. In fact, the donkey is a complete one hundred and eighty degree turn from the image of a war horse, clad in armor, with a splendid figure of a king mounted on it. The donkey in this prophecy is a sign used to signify a changing of expectation for what God has in store for his chosen people: not a mighty king, but a humble one, like his lowly mount, who has come to restore hearts, not land or title.

Jesus then fulfills this prophecy of Zechariah in Matthew 21:1–9. These verses are the biblical account of Palm Sunday, or Jesus's triumphant entry into Jerusalem, with the donkey as his chosen "war horse."

> When they drew near Jerusalem and came to Bethphage on the Mount of Olives, Jesus sent two disciples, saying to them, "Go into the village opposite you, and immediately you will find an ass tethered, and a colt with her. Untie them and bring them here to me. And if anyone should say anything to you, reply, 'The master has need of them.' Then he will send them at once." (Matt. 21:1–3)

This happened so that what had been spoken through the prophet might be fulfilled:

> Say to daughter Zion, "Behold, your king comes to you, meek and riding on an ass, and on a colt, the foal of a beast of burden." The disciples went and did as Jesus had ordered them. They brought the ass and the colt and laid their cloaks over them as he sat upon them. The very large crowd spread their cloaks on the road, while others cut branches from the trees and strewed them on the road. The crowds preceding him and those following kept crying out

and saying: "Hosanna to the Son of David; blessed
is he who comes in the name of the Lord; hosanna
in the highest." (Matt. 21:5–9)

Biblical scholar Mary Margaret Pazdan, OP, comments on
Zechariah that the Messiah will be "'meek' in his corresponding
role as servant."[4] Because the donkey is a symbol of humility and
the poor, the way in which the Messiah enters Jerusalem is an
indication of the type of king he will be.

From these two biblical texts also comes the traditional
meaning of the stripe located on the donkey's back. The donkey
was "honored by Christ, tradition says, for his triumphant ride
into Jerusalem. The dark stripe running down its back and
crossed by another at its shoulders was said to be bestowed by
Jesus, prophetic of the crucifixion, as an honorable badge for its
part in redemption."[5]

The cross on the donkey's back can also be a reminder for
Christians of our humble walk with Christ. Everywhere the
donkey goes, the cross goes with him. Like the donkey, we too
have to pick up our crosses, whatever they may be, place them on
our backs, and humbly carry them to Jesus, so that he may defeat
them as he did his own.

Donkey and Mule in the Lives of Saints

Once we learn how God has used the donkey as a humble
identifier for the coming Messiah, it should not come as a shock
that our hairy friend and his half-brother the mule are also major
characters in the history of the Church, particularly in the lives
of the saints.

St. Anthony of Padua was a Portuguese priest and Franciscan
friar during the thirteenth century. There is a famous story

involving him and a mule that takes place in the city of Bourges, France, or as some accounts say, Rimini, Italy.[6]

Anthony was known as a great miracle worker and preacher. A Jewish man by the name of Guillard would often listen to Anthony preach the Catholic faith, and though interested in what the friar had to say, he could not come to terms with the doctrine of the Real Presence of Jesus in the Eucharist. Guillard asked Anthony for a sign that would prove to him that Jesus was truly present in the Eucharist, and Anthony agreed. If God gave Guillard the sign that he asked for, he said that he would convert to the Catholic faith. With terms agreed, Anthony and Guillard devised a challenge to test the teaching of the Real Presence.

The challenge went as follows: Guillard had a mule that he would lock up in a room without food for three days. After three days, the mule would be taken to a public square in front of all the people and offered oats by Guillard. Anthony was to be carrying the sacred host in a monstrance, a transparent container used to expose and venerate the Eucharist. If the mule did not eat the oats, but instead knelt before the host, Guillard said that he would truly believe.

St. Anthony fasted and prayed for three days in preparation for the challenge. At the end of the third day, with all the town assembled, he made his way with Jesus in the Blessed Sacrament to the town square. The mule arrived famished after not touching a bite of food for three days, and before it Guillard sat a plate of oats. At the same time, Anthony held the host in front of the mule and said, "In the name of thy Creator, whose body I, though unworthy, hold in my hands, I enjoin and command thee, O being deprived of reason, to come hither instantly and prostrate thyself before thy God; so that by this sign unbelievers may know that all creation is subject to the Lamb who is daily immolated upon our altars."[7]

In the presence of its Creator, the animal set aside its want and need for food. In a gesture of reverence, the mule raised its hind legs and bent its front knees, and, in a way only a four-legged animal can, knelt before Jesus in the Eucharist. Acknowledging the miracle, Guillard was humbled by God's grace and made good on his promise to enter the Church. He also had a church built at the spot of the miracle as a commemoration of the day when God used a mule to help bring souls to Christ.[8]

If you are like me and had a difficult time imagining a mule kneeling, there is a beautiful Renaissance-era painting by Domenico Beccafumi titled *St. Anthony and the Miracle of the Mule* that accurately captures the mule's kneeling form.[9] For me, this story is a beautiful reminder that I need to drop down on my knees and thank God for the gift of his presence in my life and throw away other distractions that may take away from my time with him. If a mule that has not eaten in days is able to put away its hunger and recognize its Creator, then shouldn't I put aside all my distractions and just spend time with the Lord? The mule knew where it truly belonged, kneeling in gratitude before God.

In the life of Saint Francis of Assisi, also, a donkey was able to show the bond of friendship that can be formed between an animal and its owner. It is said that on St. Francis's deathbed, he paused to thank his donkey for carrying him throughout his life, and that his donkey wept for him.[10]

In a 2013 study conducted by The Donkey Sanctuary in Europe, experts found that donkeys have excellent memory and intelligence. "They can learn and problem-solve at the same pace as dolphins and dogs. These factors mean that donkeys remember good and bad experiences for a long time. Negative or painful experiences affect the donkey's behaviour, sometimes for years, so being a careful and considerate handler is vital."[11]

This study enlightens the relationship that St. Francis had with his donkey companion. Because donkeys learn from negative or painful experiences, this donkey's relationship with St. Francis must have been peaceful and considerate. Francis treated the donkey as his friend. Their friendship reminds us that we should be kind not just to each other, but to all of God's creatures.

One of the most common places in the lives of future saints (me and you!), that a donkey can be found in is in Christmas traditions. Popular in my home in Arkansas, and in many other places across the world, is the Christmas crèche or Nativity scene. The Nativity scene with the child Jesus lying in a manger can be traced back to the early church as early as the first century, but the way in which we experience it today was made popular by the Patron Saint of Animals, St. Francis of Assisi, on Christmas Eve in Greccio, Italy, in the year 1223. At this Christmas Eve celebration, St. Francis introduced the world to a live Nativity by incorporating an ox and a donkey to be placed on either side of the Christ child in order to reenact the birth at Bethlehem, thus giving our friend the donkey a special place in Church tradition as a witness and a warm comforter of the newborn Savior of the World.[12]

From that day in 1223 in Italy, the Nativity scene has decreased in size, but not in practice. Tiny figures of wise men, the Holy Family, sheep, oxen, and the donkey now sit underneath many of our Christmas trees, reminding us of the humble beginnings of the birth of Christ.

My family has always put up a Nativity scene in our home, and it has special meaning to me. Normally, such scenes are put up at the start of Advent, the four Sundays before Christmas when we prepare for the birth of Christ. I actually leave mine up year-round, because my mother gave each of my brothers and me a Nativity scene when we were married. Because I took about a decade or so longer than mom anticipated to wed, she had to hold on to mine for many years. I leave it out not only as a tremendous reminder of the gift of my Savior, but because, like the donkey in the Nativity scene, it reminds me to gaze lovingly at the family God has blessed me with.

A second fun Christmas tradition that includes the donkey has come to us through the lively culture of Italian Americans of the 1960s. This decade saw the dawn of a classic Christmas song called "Dominick the Donkey." Performed by singer Lou Monte, the song tells the story of a donkey that helps Santa Claus deliver Christmas presents for children in Italy.[13] Until several years ago, I had never heard it. Now when I listen to the words of a song about a humble donkey (you'll find it easily on YouTube) that does not look like a beautiful reindeer soaring through the skies on Christmas, delivering gifts of joy to all the good girls and boys, I can understand why it has become a Christmas favorite. Dominick is a perfect parallel to that humble baby, born in a manger in Bethlehem, who brought the most beautiful gift of all to us: salvation.

Donkeys in Scripture and in the lives of the saints demonstrate one of the greatest of Christian virtues: humility. For an animal that is considered by many to be goofy looking and unintelligent, this creature has played an amazing role throughout salvation history. Perhaps next time we are driving down the road and see a long-eared, buck-toothed donkey staring at us from behind a fence in a verdant pasture, we can smile and say, "Thank you."

KISS A PIG

*"I would rather believe that pigs can fly
than believe that my brethren could lie."*
—St. Thomas Aquinas

I will do just about anything for a good charity. I have been duct taped to a wall, had a pie thrown in my face, competed in a blazing hot wings food eating challenge, and even won an Oreo cookie eating contest. All these events raised money for a good cause, and though they were at times uncomfortable, I was able to endure all with cheer and a spirit of giving.

Then, one day at work, I volunteered to be in a charity kiss-a-pig contest. The person that raised the most money for the contest had to kiss a pig and was then able to donate the money raised to a charity of their choosing. To make a long story short, I raised the most money and was selected to kiss a pig. I really did not think this would be the worst type of charity punishment I have endured. I mean, pigs are cute. How bad could it be? Well, never again will I kiss a pig!

For starters, I was informed that I was going to have to kiss her on the lips instead of on top of the head, as I had planned. When the pig came into the room, she appeared to have a runny nose, as there was a wee bit of snot dripping down her slimy snout. To top it off, the pig had been eating dog food and smelled like a sack of Purina.

The big moment arrived, and the kiss happened. Sparks did not fly for either of us, and I am eternally grateful that this was not a French pig that would have further scarred me. Even the pig probably thought to herself, "Never again will I let a human kiss me!" Hopefully, many lives were saved on this day because of the charitable donation made through the uncomfortable awkwardness of man and pig.

That is probably the most memorable interaction I have ever had with a pig other than bacon, sausage, pork loin, or ribs. Salvation history is quite a different story, though, and Scripture tells of the lives of holy people throughout the ages who were involved with pigs to the glory of God.

If pigs are able to help us grow closer to God, then I will take mine with an extra side of bacon.

Pigs in the Bible

To say that pigs have a rather sordid history throughout Scripture would be an understatement. The first time we run into them in the Old Testament is in Leviticus 11:1–8, as God gives to Moses and Aaron the list of meats that are considered clean and unclean to eat or touch.

> The LORD said to Moses and Aaron: Speak to the Israelites and tell them: Of all land animals these are the ones you may eat: Any animal that has hoofs you may eat, provided it is cloven-footed and chews the cud. But you shall not eat any of the following from among those that only chew the cud or only

have hoofs: the camel, which indeed chews the cud, but does not have hoofs and is therefore unclean for you; the rock hyrax, which indeed chews the cud, but does not have hoofs and is therefore unclean for you; the hare, which indeed chews the cud, but does not have hoofs and is therefore unclean for you; and the pig, which does indeed have hoofs and is cloven-footed, but does not chew the cud and is therefore unclean for you. You shall not eat their meat, and you shall not touch their carcasses; they are unclean for you.

Many pigs were rejoicing that day in Israel! "Alleluia! Praise the Lord!" they snorted in piggy unison.

Why were some meats forbidden and others not? After spending time searching through commentaries and biblical footnotes, I found that there really is not a specific reason given that God would forbid some meats and not others.[14] Perhaps after all of the human race's disobedience to God's commands (such as Adam and Eve in the Garden, and the Israelites in the Promised Land), these restrictions were a way of simply obeying God's command and showing faithfulness. Fr. Lawrence Boadt, in *Reading the Old Testament*, put it this way: "These restrictions apply to people in everyday life and make every moment fitting for the praise of God. . . . It teaches us that the basic outlook of Israel toward food was not just to gain nourishment but to reflect God's goodness in creation."[15]

If Moses and Aaron were seen as saviors to the pigs in Israel, then Jesus must have been viewed by them as the destroyer of worlds. In Mark 7:17–23, Jesus establishes that it is not so much food or meat that can defile the heart, mind, or soul of a person, but the things that come from without.

When he got home away from the crowd his disciples questioned him about the parable. He said to them, "Are even you likewise without understanding? Do you not realize that everything that goes into a person from outside cannot defile, since it enters not the heart but the stomach and passes out into the latrine? . . . But what comes out of a person, that is what defiles. From within people, from their hearts, come evil thoughts, unchastity, theft, murder, adultery, greed, malice, deceit, licentiousness, envy, blasphemy, arrogance, folly. All these evils come from within and they defile."

With this statement, Jesus turned the Jewish purification laws upside down and seems to have declared all foods clean, consequently putting pork back on the menu, to the annoyance of pigs everywhere.

Scholar Philip Van Linden, CM, comments on Mark 7: "External things, like the food one eats, do not make a person evil. It is one's actions, inspired from within, that show when a person is not living according to God's commands. Mark hopes that his readers will look to the various ways they are living in relationship with others to see if they are responding to God 'from within' (with their whole being) or merely with 'lip service' (with superficial nods to tradition)."[16] In essence, Jesus is asking the crowd if it is more important not to eat pig or to love your neighbor. Evil thoughts, unchastity, theft, murder, adultery, greed, malice, deceit, licentiousness, envy, blasphemy, arrogance, and folly do not come from eating pigs. They come from whether or not we are truly living God's commandments.

This story is always a gut check for me, because I am at times scrupulous and worry that God is following me around making a list of what I do wrong. It is often hard to acknowledge (by what I do, not necessarily what I say) that I am *not* in control of my salvation and that God is in command. I worry, did I say the right thing to that person? Did I pray the Rosary and not have my mind wander? Why did I think those horrible thoughts? These are not things that God is making a list of to punish or condemn me. God is searching my heart, seeing the love that is within for others, and smiling at the beauty that shines forth. Though it is good to do those things, I know that God wants me to trust in his mercy, not worry, and spread that beautiful love to others that is in my heart.

There is another story in Scripture that I am always left slightly perplexed about: the healing of the Gerasene demoniac, found in Mark chapter 5. In this story, there is a man possessed by an unclean spirit who lives in the tombs by the sea in Gerasa, a non-Jewish territory. This Gerasene man goes about the tombs crying out loud and harming himself night and day. People in the area try to shackle him and subdue him, but the man is so strong he breaks the shackles apart and continues to bring harm to himself.

Mark 5:6–14 says,

> Catching sight of Jesus from a distance, he ran up and prostrated himself before him, crying out in a loud voice, "What have you to do with me, Jesus, Son of the Most High God? I adjure you by God, do not torment me!" (He had been saying to him, "Unclean spirit, come out of the man!") He asked him, "What is your name?" He replied, "Legion is my name. There are many of us." And he pleaded earnestly with him not to drive them away from that territory.

Now a large herd of swine was feeding there on the hillside. And they pleaded with him, "Send us into the swine. Let us enter them." And he let them, and the unclean spirits came out and entered the swine. The herd of about two thousand rushed down a steep bank into the sea, where they were drowned. The swineherds ran away and reported the incident in the town and throughout the countryside. And people came out to see what had happened.

As I said earlier in the chapter, the pigs of Israel must have seen Jesus as the destroyer of worlds. First, he says they are okay to eat, and next he is sending unclean spirits into them and they are running off a cliff! If I were a pig in Israel, I would have steered clear of Jesus of Nazareth.

Though they met a sad end, the pigs are not the point of the Gospel story. The mercy that Jesus shows upon the non-Jewish man, now healed, and in his right mind, shows all in the area of Gerasa that the gospel is for Jew and non-Jew alike. All nations and people are invited to the banquet of Jesus.[17]

How is a story of the death of two thousand pigs considered a "remarkable miracle"? Watching a herd of pink, chubby, snorting boars, sows, and piglets stampede off a cliff would have been horrible to observe and experience. However, in a macabre sort of salvific beauty, watching an animal considered unclean, foreign, and sinful run off a cliff may also call to mind an image of sin being cast into the abyss for everyone on earth. We must simply come and ask for this mercy from the Savior who commands and defeats this sin for all.

Pigs in the Lives of Saints

The presence of pigs in the lives of Catholic saints also stretches back centuries. There are many instances when God has used the pig through his saints to bring about conversions, miracles, and answers to countless prayers.

Every year on the third of February, for instance, we celebrate the Feast of St. Blaise, the fourth-century patron saint of throat diseases. In churches throughout the world, two candles are placed across the throat of the faithful in the popular tradition of blessing the throat. The reason for this tradition of blessing throats using two candles is in part due to a pig.

In this story, Blaise is arrested for being a Christian and taken to a prison in Sebastea (modern-day Turkey). On the way to prison, Blaise comes across an old woman whose pig has been carried off by a wolf. Hearing the woman's pleas to help her recover the animal, Blaise commands the wolf to return the pig to the woman. The wolf obliges and returns the pig uninjured. Then, when Blaise reaches the prison in Sebastea, this same woman brings him two candles to light the darkness of his prison cell. Because of the miracle of the pig, and the many cures of throat diseases by St. Blaise, the rite of blessing of throats is now carried out with two wax candles.[18]

Every year when I was growing up, my small Catholic parish in Charleston, Arkansas, celebrated the feast of St. Blaise and the blessing of the throats. We would all gather in line as if we were going to receive Communion, and as we arrived at the front of the church, a minister or priest would place two wax candles around our throats and say, "Through the intercession of St. Blaise, bishop and martyr, may God deliver you from every disease of the throat and from every other illness: In the name of the Father, and of the Son, and of the Holy Spirit."[19] I was happy to receive the blessing, but I had no idea why candles were involved. It turns out, they were a gift from someone to light someone else's darkest hours because of the kindness shown to a woman and her pig. God's creatures matter, and when we show them love, we are sometimes radiating that love to others, as in the case of St. Blaise and the woman whose pig was stolen by a wolf.

Pigs have also been included in the life history of St. Brigid of Kildare. This sixth-century patroness of Ireland is said to have been able to tame wild animals, including, in one story, a wild boar. In this legend, several hunters are said to have been chasing a boar through the wilderness. The boar ended up running into Brigid's convent, where the hunters were unable to follow. The hunters were forced to halt at the gate and wait for the saint to release the boar back into the wild, where it would make for an easy kill.

Brigid, however, had different plans. Noticing the boar was exhausted, and having pity upon it, she sent word to the hunters that the boar had claimed the right of sanctuary inside the convent just as humans could do and was now under the church's protection. St. Brigid then cared for the boar and released it into her own herd, where it became tame and lived the rest of its life.[20]

I am often amazed at these stories, in which wild animals seem to have an instinctual knowledge to seek out a holy person in times of trouble. Whether by sheer luck, or something greater, somehow this boar ended up in the care of a saint and its life was spared. If animals flee to the holy when they are in trouble, we have to ask ourselves, are we doing the same?

Another story involving a pig comes to us from *The Little Flowers of Saint Francis of Assisi*. This book tells the story of the first Franciscans, who went about their world spreading the gospel. One of these adventures involves a friar named Brother Juniper and his zeal to help a sick brother of his order.

One day, Brother Juniper traveled to visit a sick brother in a neighboring area. Upon seeing the sick brother, Juniper was overcome with love to help and asked him if he could do anything. The sick brother replied, "You would do me a great pleasure if you could get me a pig's foot to eat." This brother must have been really craving barbeque to make such a request. Juniper immediately ran off to a forest, where many pigs were eating, and cut off a pig's foot, leaving the pig in the pasture, running off to prepare the morsel for the sick brother to eat. Juniper is said to have prepared the pig's foot with great love and kindness, and the sick brother is supposed to have eaten it with enthusiasm.

Juniper was so happy that he was able to help the sick man, that he did not even consider the consequences of his actions. Then came the pig's owner to the friary to ask for recompense for his injured pig. The Franciscans tried to repay the man, but he would have nothing of it. Instead, he went about fuming and yelling in the neighboring area and villages about what thieves the Franciscans were. St. Francis called Juniper to him and commanded him out of holy obedience to seek out the man and ask forgiveness. Juniper did as Francis asked, and begged forgiveness of the farmer. The farmer's heart was warmed with Juniper's love for his fellow man, and he in turn ended up asking the Franciscans forgiveness for all he had been saying about them. As reparation, he donated the rest of the pig for them to eat.[21]

Granted, this story is morbid from the pig's perspective. However, Juniper was so full of the Holy Spirit and love that there was nothing he would not do for his sick brother. Juniper only wanted to please his brother and bring him some consolation from his illness, so it did not matter to Juniper what he was asked to do. He probably would have offered his life for his sick friend to become better. Next time we are in a gas station, and we see a nasty-looking jar of pickled pig's feet on the counter next to the cash register, may we remember the love Juniper showed to his neighbor and maybe give someone hungry near us a smile and buy them a pig's foot.

A last anecdote about pigs in history and tradition concerns the patron saint of swineherds, St. Anthony the Abbot. Anthony is sometimes called the Father of Monks. In his life, he is said to have healed people suffering from various skin diseases. Because of this, he is often portrayed in art as having a pig standing next to him, because pig fat was also used in the fourth century to treat certain skin diseases. Pig farmers would see Anthony and a pig together in a painting or a statue, and therefore they made him their patron saint.[22]

With all of these wonderful stories and tales of pigs throughout the Bible and Christian history, it is no wonder so many people hold them in such high regard. In fact, one of the most famous Catholic authors of the twentieth century, G. K. Chesterton, admired and wrote very eloquently about the pig. In an article published by the *Illustrated London News* on May 8, 1909, Chesterton had the following to say:

> I never could imagine why pigs should not be kept as pets. To begin with, pigs are very beautiful animals. Those who think otherwise are those who do not look at anything with their own eyes, but only through other people's eyeglasses. The actual lines of a pig (I mean of a really fat pig) are among the loveliest and most luxuriant in nature; the pig has the same great curves, swift and yet heavy, which we see in the rushing water or in rolling cloud. Compared to him, the horse, for instance, is a bony, angular, and

abrupt animal. I remember that Mr. H. G. Wells, in arguing for the relativity of things (a subject over which even the Greek philosophers went to sleep until Christianity woke them up), pointed out that, while a horse is commonly beautiful if seen in profile, he is excessively ugly if seen from the top of a dog-cart, having a long, lean neck, and a body like a fiddle. Now, there is no point of view from which a really corpulent pig is not full of sumptuous and satisfying curves. You can look down on a pig from the top of the most unnaturally lofty dog-cart; and I suppose a dog-cart has as much to do with pigs as it has with dogs. You can examine the pig from the top of an omnibus, from the top of the Monument, from a balloon, or an air-ship; and as long as he is visible he will be beautiful. In short, he has that fuller, subtler, and more universal kind of shapeliness which the unthinking (gazing at pigs and distinguished journalists) mistake for a mere absence of shape. For fatness really is a valuable quality.[23]

Seldom in the annals of world history, not just salvation history, has one author seemed to put so much thought and energy into describing a pig. May the words of the Bible, the stories of Catholic saints, and Mr. Chesterton always remind us that pigs are just another beautiful example of how God uses creation to speak to us in ways we cannot even begin to understand or comprehend.

OF MICE AND MARRIAGE

*"I only hope that we don't lose sight of one thing—
that it was all started by a mouse."*
—WALT DISNEY

My wife and I fell in love because of a mice infestation. Dating can be awkward at times, and sometimes even getting a date can seem impossible—this is part of the never-ending saga of the constantly asked question, *When will I meet that special someone to spend the rest of my life with?* My heart was plagued with all of these doubts and fears until the summer of 2013, when I met my wife for the first time.

Christy was hired as the new cheerleading coach at our high school, and on the first day of our summer professional development she was assigned to sit at my table and be a part of my group. No doubt, the first time we met, she was immediately in love with me. I decided, however, that I would take things slowly. So, we talked at the table, and then again in passing several times after that meeting, as the school year progressed. I began to think that maybe this woman was someone I would like to ask out. My only problem was, how do I ask her?

Thankfully, her office became infested with mice. Their droppings and trash were everywhere: on her desk, on her papers, on her keyboard, and in her filing cabinet. When I found out about this horrible turn of events, I cheered with joy, because I knew that this was my chance to win her heart. Capitalizing on an unfortunate set of circumstances, I sent a message and asked if she wanted me to bring my cat, Anastasia, to stay in her office overnight and take care of her mouse problem. Much to Anastasia's chagrin, she was not allowed in Christy's office, but love blossomed forth from that message and the rest is history. Thank you, God, for mice infestations!

Mice in the Bible

Finding mice in Scripture can be as difficult as finding them hiding in your home, office, or place of work. Mentions of them are very few, and they do not make a lot of noise in the larger stories of the Bible. Every now and again, though, we catch sight of them in the background if we choose to turn on the light and look.

The first mention of a rat or a mouse in the Bible is in the book of Leviticus 11:29, as one of the animals considered unclean in Israel's Laws of Ritual Purity. "Of the creatures that swarm on the ground, the following are unclean for you: the rat, the mouse . . ." In fact, not only are mice considered unclean, but also the prophet Isaiah hammers home just how forbidden they are as he mentions them separately after pigs and other "abominable things" in Isaiah 66:17. "Those who sanctify and purify themselves to go into the gardens, following one who stands within, eating pig's flesh, abominable things, and mice, shall all together come to an end, with their deeds and purposes—oracle of the LORD."

The theologian Fr. William Most comments on this passage that "those who seem to flourish without God will be burned down by the Lord. Such wicked persons go into the garden and do what they call 'purifying' themselves to worship false gods, and they follow a leader who even eats the flesh of pigs and rats and does other abominable things."[24] Those who flourish without God will be brought low. The mouse here can serve as a reminder to us that in the Kingdom of God, the natural order is turned over on its head. Those who are considered strong, wealthy, and powerful (the mice eaters in this verse), do not enter into heaven. It is those who do not worship false idols, are humble, and are faithful to God and his commands (the people not eating mice) who will see eternal life.

I have eaten and heard about people eating many strange creatures in my life. My mother likes to tell the story of my grandfather killing a possum and then wanting my grandmother to cook it for dinner. My grandmother did as requested, but after the meal she threw away every pot and plate the animal touched. I have even heard a horrendous tale from a friend from Louisiana of him and his friends making an armadillo étouffée one evening.

Mice, though, are one thing I have never tried or heard of people trying to eat. When we hear about people in biblical times eating mice, and the fact that it was forbidden by the purity laws to consume them, one would think that this would be an easy task to follow. However, just like the people from these ancient times who knew eating a mouse was forbidden, we too know that some sins are forbidden by God and yet we choose to partake of them. God always has our best interests in heart. When he and the Church teach us about sin, it is so we may have life in him, live to the fullest, and reach our true potential. So, put down that mouse sandwich, or whatever sinful habit may be keeping you from God, and trust in the Lord.

In the first book of Samuel chapters 4–6, mice played a huge part in helping Israel reclaim something precious that was lost to them, the Ark of the Covenant. These chapters tell the story of a battle between the Israelites and the Philistines at Ebenezer. The Israelites lost this battle and in the process lost the Ark of the Covenant, which is said to have contained the Ten Commandments given to Moses by God on Mount Sinai, manna from the time of the Israelite exodus in the desert, and the staff of Aaron. The Philistines then took the Ark to Ashdod, where they kept it in the home of one of their false gods, Dagon.

It is said that the hand of the Lord lay heavy upon the people of Ashdod, and mice infested their fields and brought forth tumors, a symptom of the plague. The disease ravaged the Philistines, and after having the Ark in their possession for several months, they decided they were ready to give it back to the Israelites. To make reparation to God for taking the Ark, the Philistines had images of five golden tumors and five golden mice made to represent the five cities and the five leaders of the Philistines who were afflicted by the plague and to give glory to the God of Israel. Then, with the golden mice and tumors, they sent that Ark back, hoping that through this act, God might relieve them of their affliction and heal them.

Biblical scholar Paula J. Bowes comments, "The Philistines know enough Israelite history to see a parallel between this event and the plagues brought on the Egyptians before the Exodus, and they are determined not to repeat the Pharaoh's stubbornness nor its consequences. In a kind of sympathetic magic, they shape their conciliatory gifts of gold into five hemorrhoids and five mice, one for each of their cities."[25] The Philistines realized that if they kept the Ark any longer, they might end up worse than the Egyptians, who had ten plagues unleashed upon them as described in the book of Exodus. Though the golden mice seemed like a nice gesture, they showed that the Philistines, like Pharaoh, did not fully comprehend the power of God over life and death. The golden mice did not buy healing and forgiveness. It is only the love, compassion, and mercy of God that can heal us.

Mice in the Lives of Saints

Mice in the lives of Catholic saints can best be described as incredibly tense, at times, good and wholesome, at others, and then sometimes, rather morose.

Saint Gerard Mejalla was an Italian lay brother in the Redemptorist order during the 1700s. He was widely considered a miracle worker and brought many people to the Catholic faith during his holy life.

One day, while walking along a highway, Gerard came across a farmer in distress. Mice had come into his field and destroyed his crop, which was the only means of support of his family. Gerard asked the farmer if he would rather the mice die or go elsewhere, and the farmer answered that he would rather they die. So Gerard raised his hand and made the sign of the cross over the field. At that instant, the ground became covered with dead mice. The farmer was overcome with joy at the miracle, though the same could hardly be said for the mice.[26]

Before we jump to conclusions and judge St. Gerard as the worst rodent hitman in the history of the Catholic Church, remember that he was asking the farmer what he would like done. If we were in a similar situation, and mice came into our home, the first reaction we would normally have is to buy traps to kill them. If the mice went elsewhere, they could have destroyed another farmer's crop, causing a family to starve, or return to the original farm to do even more damage. I like to use this story not as an excuse to kill mice, but to reflect on how I sometimes need to be patient and understand a situation before jumping to conclusions. For example, the other day at school, I thought students were skipping my math class. I found myself getting angry and frustrated that my students would ever even consider doing this. Then I discovered that they were not skipping but had missed my class because they were competing at a science fair.

It is awful that all the mice were killed in this tale, but how many families and their property were also saved because of the farmer's decision? It is impossible to know the mind of God, and these mice help me to understand that fact, and trust in his will.

In a related note, if you or someone you love are suffering from mice or pest infestation, I found a prayer that you can say to hopefully rid yourself or another of the situation. "Graciously hear our prayers, we beseech You, O Lord, that we who are justly punished for our sins and must bear the punishment of this plague, may be freed from it for the glory of Your name. By Your power may these injurious animals be driven off so that they will do no harm to anyone and will leave our fields and meadows unharmed, and so that the things sprouting and growing in these fields may honor Your majesty and serve our needs. Amen."[27]

A much more joyful encounter with mice takes place in Peru in the seventeenth century. There are many stories of St. Martin De Porres, a holy Dominican friar, caring for and loving mistreated animals in his city. In one, a brother of Martin's walks into a kitchen to find Martin watching a dog and a cat eating from the same food bowl at his feet. The friar was about to call the other brothers to come witness this extraordinary incident, when the two friars saw a mouse stick its head out of a hole in a nearby wall. Martin looked at the mouse and said, "Don't be afraid, little one. If you're hungry, come and eat with the others." The little mouse scampered hesitantly to the food bowl and ate peacefully with the other two animals.[28]

In this beautiful story, we see that God is able to overcome the natural order of predator versus prey and let all species live together peacefully. In the presence of the holy, in this case St. Martin, his love and peace radiates to others around him. In this instance, those around him were a cat, a mouse, and a dog. Also, his words to the mouse, "Don't be afraid, little one. If you're hungry, come and eat with the others," can be said to all of us who consider ourselves too small to do anything for the Kingdom of God. All of us, no matter how small, are invited to the table to eat with the others, and we all matter to God.

As we can see, the mouse may be small, but it is not exactly as quiet as "a church mouse" when viewed in Scripture and the history of the saints. Though most of the stories label mice as pests, unclean, and harbingers of death, they can still give us small insights into our spiritual lives. For example, we can get along with others, as the mouse did in the story of St. Martin de Porres, and we can learn from the stories of the Old Testament and follow God's commands. Also, in my case, God can even use a mouse infestation to become an answer to a long-awaited prayer, a prayer to finally go on a date with my future wife.

THE FISH FRIES OF MEN

"God is closer to us than water is to a fish."
—St. Catherine of Siena

T he sun rises lazily in the eastern horizon. The light begins to paint a celestial canvas of pink, orange, purple, and yellow hues, giving even a brightness to the dark clouds that have yet to be banished from the previous night's storm. The temperature is chilly for a Friday morning in early March, but then again, March comes in like a lion and goes out like a lamb.

An old Ford pickup truck pulls into a seemingly abandoned church parking lot while the sun finishes its game of peekaboo with the horizon line to shine brightly upon the earth below it. A Chevy pickup then pulls up, then a Dodge, then another Ford, then a Toyota, then a Nissan, followed by several more makes and models of minivans and automobiles. Out of these vehicles step men of the Knights of Columbus. It is a Friday of Lent, and most Catholics know what that means: today, there will be a Knights of Columbus fish fry!

Igloo and Yeti coolers begin to be unloaded from the beds of the pickups. "First the beer, then the fish," one of the knights says to another. After the beer is placed lovingly in a convenient spot next to the fish fryer, the fillets of catfish are then breaded and prepared in a specific way according to the recipes passed down from one knight to another from generations past. In fact, some knights would rather eat their catfish raw than give up this beloved recipe of culinary delight.

After the cooking of the fish is finally completed the time has come to feed the multitudes, Catholics and non-Catholics alike, from surrounding towns and communities in the area. One cannot help noting the connection between the feeding of the hungry crowds and Jesus, who in the Gospel multiplied fish and loaves of bread to feed great crowds. The people begin to eat and they are filled. The knights have achieved their goals: they have made money for charitable endeavors in the Church and they have satiated the masses. This deserves another round, men! Well done, my good and faithful servants!

Fish in the Bible

Not only do fish taste amazing, but they may also be the most interesting and exciting animals to read about in the Scriptures. They multiply, help restore sight to the blind, and feed the resurrected Savior of the world. In the other chapters of this book, most animals represent a specific trait or virtue, such as strength and power. Fish, on the other hand, have become symbols of certain Bible figures because of their interaction with them throughout salvation history.

One such person is Tobit. His rather fishy story is from the book of Tobit, which is found in every Catholic Bible. In this book, the Archangel Raphael instructs Tobiah on how to live past his wedding night by burning a fish heart and liver, as well as on how to restore sight to his blind father, Tobit, by using fish gall.

In the story, Tobiah is marrying Sarah, who has been married seven times before, but on each one of her wedding nights, a demon has come into her bridal chamber and killed her husband. Tobiah's father also has a problem, as he was outside sleeping in a courtyard one evening and bird droppings fell into his eyes, resulting in blindness. To prevent a wedding day massacre from happening once again, and to restore sight to Tobiah's father, the Archangel Raphael tells Tobiah, "Slit the fish open and take out its gall, heart, and liver, and keep them with you; but throw away the other entrails. Its gall, heart, and liver are useful for medicine." Tobiah does this; he puts aside the gall, heart, and liver. He roasts and eats part of the fish; the rest he salts and keeps for the journey. Then the young man asks the angel: "Brother Azariah [Raphael], what medicine is in the fish's heart, liver, and gall?"

The angel answers Tobiah: "As for the fish's heart and liver, if you burn them to make smoke in the presence of a man or a woman who is afflicted by a demon or evil spirit, any affliction will flee and never return. As for the gall, if you apply it to the eyes of one who has white scales, blowing right into them, sight will be restored" (Tobit 6:5–9). Tobiah does exactly as instructed: fish gall is blown into Tobit's eyes, and the liver and heart are burned on the wedding night. As a result, the demon flees, there is no wedding day massacre, and Tobit's sight is restored.

Scripture scholar Irene Nowell, OSB, comments, "Water as a source of life and death is a common biblical image. . . . [W]hen Tobiah follows Raphael's instruction, seizes the fish, and saves its gall, heart, and liver, it becomes a source of healing."[29] In other words, the fish came from the water, a source of life, created by

God. God then chose to work through his creation to restore life to three different people, and all he used were the insides of a fish.

I have often tried to cook fish in my home, but as in the above story, the stench is always overpowering and lingers afterwards for days at a time. I am probably not preparing or cooking the fish correctly, and as with the demon, the stench makes me want to flee to the nearest hotel room to wait out the foul odor until it finally abates.

However, the fish entrails in the story of Tobit can teach us the importance of obedience to God and his commandments. Obedience to God brings life and salvation to people. The characters in Tobit obeyed the angel's fishy commands, were saved, and were able to live their lives more fully, as God wants all of us to do. In the cases of Tobiah and Sarah, the noxious smell of a fish's liver and heart became an act of obedience to God that produced a type of odor of sanctity in their situation, allowing God's hand to protect them and allow a long-awaited love story to finally take place. Likewise, fish gall rubbed in the eyes of Tobit restored sight to this once-blind man. So perhaps next time we are in a restaurant, and we detect a pungent fishy smell coming from the kitchen, instead of crinkling our nose and turning our head, we should inhale deeply the smelly reminder that God loves us and wants us to live and see with the beauty of the eyes of faith.

But Tobit does not contain the most famous fish story in the Bible. That would have to be the one involving Jonah.

Notice I did not say whale. The Bible never says that Jonah was swallowed into the belly of a whale. Jonah 2:1 states, "But the LORD sent a great fish to swallow Jonah, and he remained in the belly of the fish three days and three nights." Fish.

Why was Jonah in the fish's belly for three days and three nights? The book of Jonah says that God called Jonah to go preach to the Ninevites in order to have them repent of their sins. Jonah wanted nothing to do with this task given to him by God, so he went and bought a ticket on a ship to flee far away from Nineveh. However, Jonah did not take into account that it is difficult to run from God, and the ship that Jonah was sailing on was caught up in a great storm.

In order to make travel through the storm easier, the men on the ship decided to throw some things overboard to lighten the load, so as to better navigate the huge waves. One of the things they threw overboard was Jonah. While he was in the water, a great fish swallowed him, and in its belly he stayed for three days and three nights. Jonah prayed and prayed to be saved from this predicament. God heard his prayer, and the fish vomited him onto dry land. Then, again God asked Jonah to go to Nineveh and preach to the Ninevites. This time, Jonah accepted!

Irene Nowell calls the book of Jonah "the image of the all-powerful Creator who commissions the prophet and pursues him until he accepts."[30] The idea of a man being swallowed and living inside a fish for three days and three nights seems incredibly hard to imagine. However, the giant fish in this story shows us that you cannot run from God. He will never cease chasing after us to bring us closer to his heart and to the life he wants us to live. If he is looking for you, he will find you, and he may use the smelly insides of a fish as a way to finally get your attention. All created beings are subject to the Creator, including giant, prophet-swallowing fish.

In the New Testament, we see how fish begin to be linked as a symbol for Jesus and his ministry. One story in particular is found in the Gospel of Mark, chapter 8:1–10, when Jesus multiplied the loaves and fish to feed four thousand people, and in all four of the Gospels when he multiplied the loaves and the fish, once again, to feed five thousand people. Being able to feed that many people with a few fish and loaves of bread is certainly miraculous, but one of the key elements of this story is that each time the people ate, they were satisfied, a foreshadowing of Jesus and the Eucharist.

For those not familiar with the Catholic teaching on the Eucharist, the *Catechism of the Catholic Church* says this in paragraph 1324: "The Eucharist is 'the source and summit of the Christian life.' 'The other sacraments, and indeed all ecclesiastical ministries and works of the apostolate, are bound up with the Eucharist and are oriented toward it. For in the blessed Eucharist is contained the whole spiritual good of the Church, namely Christ himself, our Pasch.' "[31] To summarize, Jesus is contained body, blood, soul, and divinity in the Eucharist.

Scripture scholar Daniel J. Harrington confirms this when he says, "The feeding was viewed as an anticipation or preview of the Last Supper and thus of the Church's celebration of the Eucharist."[32] Because of the feeding of the multitudes, fish are now forever linked as a symbol for Jesus and for early Christians.

A second time fish are used to foreshadow Jesus in the Eucharist is in the book of John, chapter 21. This story occurs after the Resurrection and involves Jesus's disciples, who were on a fishing trip. After a night of fishing, the disciples are returning to the shore when they see a man on the beach. It is Jesus, but they do not recognize him yet. Jesus tells them to cast their nets on the right side of the boat. They obey his word and catch a great multitude: one hundred fifty-three, to be exact. The disciples then recognize that it is Jesus. The lightly clad Peter even jumps in headfirst to swim to him. When they get to the shore, Jesus has a fire going and asks for some fish to eat. He invites the disciples to eat with him and gives them fish and bread. An experience with the resurrected Christ is to share a meal with him, and that meal is the Eucharist.

In all of these instances where Jesus is engaged with meals with his disciples and others, fish are present as a compass pointing to the Eucharistic meal we will eventually share with him. This is why for thousands of years the fish has been a symbol of Jesus and Christianity.

Fish in the Lives of Saints

Fish have been swimming through Scripture not only throughout the history of Christianity, but also in the everyday lives of the saints. In some cases, they aid in miraculous events, but in others they help Christians strengthen their faith and love for Christ.

First, fish were used as a symbol for Christians during the second century. The letters ICHTHYS spell "fish" in Greek, and its letters were an acronym for "Jesus Christ, Son of God, Savior."[33] In this way, for the Christians the acronym became an early form of creed and a prayer. Today, in a similar way, Christians often continue this creed by placing a fish symbol on the back of their automobile, thus witnessing their faith to the world.

To be a Christian in the second century was oftentimes a death sentence. As Philip Kolowski writes, "Fish were a common part of Mediterranean life and religion, so for Christians under persecution, the Ichthys became a covert sign to identify their beliefs."[34] Christians were able to identify one another through the fish symbol without giving themselves away to those seeking to kill them.

In the year 1348, fish were responsible for saving several Eucharistic hosts. In the town of Alboraya-Almacera, Spain, a priest was carrying a ciborium with the Eucharist to several sick people in the area. In order to get to the people, the priest had to cross a river on the back of a mule. While crossing the river, he was swept off the mule by an oncoming wave. The Sacred Hosts fell out of the ciborium and were swept down the river with the current. The priest was very upset by this turn of events, but his sorrow soon turned to joy when he suddenly heard several fishermen calling him from downstream, telling him there were several fish sticking their heads out of the water with discs in their mouth. The priest ran to the place the fishermen were indicating, and sure enough, there were the three fish presenting the hosts to the priest to be given to the sick in the town. The priest returned the hosts to the ciborium and was able to deliver the precious cargo to the people.[35]

This Eucharistic miracle story calls to mind the story of Jonah in the belly of the fish and the story in Matthew 17:27 of Peter taking a coin out of a fish's mouth to pay the temple tax. In both stories, God uses fish, which have no arms or legs, to bring something important to someone or somewhere. When we think of our deficiencies and how God surely can't use us to do anything important, remember all the things he has done with only the fish and their mouths. Most of us have our arms and legs; imagine the good we can carry to one another.

Another wonderful story of fish involves St. Anthony of Padua. In the town of Rimini, Italy, there were a great many heretics gathered around to listen to Anthony preach. For days and days, Anthony proclaimed the Scriptures and the Catholic faith to them, but they chose to remain unmoved by his words.

Anthony then went to a local river by the sea and began to speak a sermon to the fish located there. He said, "Hear the word of God, you fishes of the sea and stream, since heretics and infidels are loath to listen to it." It is said that after these words, a great many fish of all shapes and sizes held their heads out of the water and listened to the saint preach. Anthony said to them:

> My brothers the fish, you are greatly bound, so long as you live, to thank your Creator that he has given you so noble an element for your habitation, because at your pleasure you have fresh waters and salt, and he has given you many shelters against storms. He has given you a clear and lucid element, and food by which you may live. God, your courteous and benign Creator, when he created you, commanded you to grow and multiply. He gave you his blessing. Then when the great flood swallowed up the world, and all the other animals were destroyed, God preserved you only without injury or harm. . . . To you it was granted, by God's command, to preserve the prophet Jonah. . . . You were the food of the everlasting King Christ Jesus before the Resurrection, and again after it, by a strange mystery. For these things, you are greatly bound to praise and bless God.

In a reverent gesture, the fish began to open their mouths and bow their heads. Anthony, filled with joy, cried out, "Blessed be the eternal God, since fishes of the water honor him far more than heretics, and the unreasoning beasts more readily heed his word than faithless people."[36] The heretics, after seeing this miracle and opening their hearts to the preaching of St. Anthony, repented and converted to the faith.

In contemplating this miracle, I realize that like Anthony, I talk to animals a lot. I talk to cats, dogs, birds. Even though they may not turn their heads and listen to me intently, my words and how I treat them can still be an example of how to love God's creation and to take care of this precious gift that he has given to us. This in itself can be a way to preach to those around us, and we never know, God may even soften someone's heart to listen to our faith.

The most well-known place that includes fish in the church of the twenty-first century is abstaining from meat on Fridays of Lent. This leads to a lot of fish eating and, as noted earlier, Knights of Columbus fish fries. Why do Catholics not eat meat on Friday? The answer is quite simple. This is a small sacrifice that we make to honor the day on which Christ was crucified, the day in which he sacrificed all for us.[37]

Abstinence from meat on Fridays led McDonald's to create the Filet-O-Fish sandwich. In Cincinnati, during the 1960s, a local McDonald's owner noticed that he was only pulling in about $75 on Fridays during Lent. He learned that many of his clientele were Catholic, and on Fridays during Lent, they were going to other places to eat because he did not have a non-meat option on the menu. He added a fish sandwich to his menu, and the rest is history.[38]

The stories and history of fish in Scripture and our faith are a remarkable gift from God. They have influenced the lives of some of the greatest saints in church history, as well as representing Christ himself and others like Tobit. Though fish can be smelly, slimy, ugly, and frustratingly hard to catch, they have still been used by God to strengthen our faith and draw others to Christ. If God can do that with a fish, what can he do with you?

DON'T STOP BELIEVING

"The Sasquatch is the strongest animal on the planet."
—ANONYMOUS

One summer evening as I sat on my couch watching television, a news story came across the screen. The reporter was talking with a man about an upcoming Bigfoot meeting being held in my town that very night. According to the report, this was a meeting of people who believe in or have had an encounter with Bigfoot in their lives. At first, I laughed at the report and probably muttered something about people being crazy, because I do not believe in Bigfoot. I think that if Bigfoot did exist, we would have found some type of fossil record or at least come across real camera footage of one in the wild. However, as I watched the news report, an unexplainable excitement grew within me and a great desire to attend this meeting. Plus, my wife was out of town and I was bored. So, I got up, put on my best clothes, and headed to the meeting, not quite knowing what to expect.

When I arrived at the mom and pop steakhouse in town that was hosting the gathering, I was absolutely taken aback by how many people had come. Every table was full of people eating, talking, and sharing stories of their encounters with the creature. Unable to find a table, many people, including me, stood up against a wall, as a plethora of dead animal heads watched over the room above us, suggesting that if Bigfoot ever did stand still for long, its head too would grace this morbid wall of death. As I listened and searched the faces of the crowd, I could not keep a smile from spreading across my face: there had to be a hundred or more people attending a Bigfoot meeting in my small hometown!

One area of the restaurant boasted a hastily put together traveling Bigfoot museum that showed grainy pictures, sighting locations of the elusive creature, and a full-size cardboard cutout. Best of all, fans could purchase bumper stickers, posters, photos, figurines, shirts, stuffed animals, and hats featuring Bigfoot silhouettes in various poses and positions.

One of the meeting workers must have noticed how much I was enjoying myself. He sauntered up and asked, "Are you a believer?"

"I beg your pardon," I said.

"Are you a believer?" he asked me again with a crazy gleam in his eyes. A realization then dawned on me that he was not asking if I were a believer in Jesus, but a believer in Bigfoot. I laughed and said, "No." He then looked at me with a terribly serious, straight face and said, "Well, I am, and I judge you. We have proof!" He then took me over to a glass case in which a footprint of Bigfoot was said to be enclosed. This looked like no other footprint I have ever laid eyes on, and looked to be very fake. I laughed again and walked off from the man, leaving him to his proof and failed attempt at proselytization.

About a minute later, an announcement was made that testimonials would be starting soon. *Oh my goodness*, I thought, *all these people are serious!* I decided it would be in my best interest to get out of there and head home before I was escorted off the premises by one of the many shotguns lying in the back of the numerous trucks in the parking lot. But that meeting was one of the greatest ten minutes of my life!

This will come as a surprise to some readers, but mythical animals are present in the Bible. Scripture actually mentions and describes several mythical animals. However, finding them depends on which translation of the Bible you are reading.

Mythical Animals in the Bible

Bigfoot is mentioned indirectly over seven hundred times in the Bible! Just kidding, but in the King James Version and the Catholic Douay-Rheims Bible, we find mention of a unicorn. Unicorns in the Bible? Psalm 91:11 in the Douay-Rheims Bible says, "But my horn shall be exalted like that of the unicorn." The same verse in the King James in Psalm 92:10 also uses the word unicorn. They are translating the Hebrew word *re'em*. A biblical scholar helps to explain: this "word is translated sometimes in our Douay-Rheims by rhinoceros (Numbers 23:22; 24:8; Deuteronomy 33:17; Job 39:9, 10), sometimes by unicorn (Psalm 21:22; 28:6; 91:11; Isaiah 34:7). That the *re'em*, far from being unicorn, was a two-horned animal, is suggested by Psalm 22, and forcibly evidenced by Deuteronomy 33:17, where its horns represent the two tribes of Ephraim and Manasses."[39]

Psalm 90 of the Douay-Rheims Bible, verse 13, speaks of another mythical creature known as the basilisk. "Thou shalt walk upon the asp and the basilisk: and thou shalt trample under foot the lion and the dragon." You may be familiar with the basilisk from horror movies or *Harry Potter and the Chamber of Secrets*. In these movies and stories, the basilisk is a gigantic snake that is able to kill you if you look directly into its eyes. These movies are not far from the mythical creature described throughout salvation history. In fact, in his article "The Biblical and Christian Roots of the Basilisk," Philip Kosloski points out that a Catholic saint, Isidore of Seville, even wrote about this evil creature as a real animal in one of his books:

> Basilisk (*basiliscus*) is a Greek word, translated into Latin as "little king". . . . because it is the king of the snakes, so that they flee when they see it because it kills them with its odor – it also kills a human if it looks at one. Indeed no flying bird may pass unharmed by the basilisk's face, but however distant it may be it is burnt up and devoured by this animal's mouth. However, the basilisk may be overcome by weasels. For this reason people take weasels into caves where the basilisk lies hidden; and as the basilisk takes flight at the sight, the weasel chases it down and kills it. Thus the Creator of nature sets forth nothing without a remedy.[40]

Despite these wonderful descriptions and exciting tales, biblical scholars point out that the basilisk we find in Psalm 90 of the Douay-Rheims Bible is only "an equivalent for several Hebrew names of snakes."[41] Despite this rather uneventful explanation, we can still learn a lot from St. Isidore's description. Isidore explains that God puts nothing in nature without great thought and care, and no darkness is too evil to be defeated by him. What a consolation this is for us if we are struggling with any temptations or troubles that we cannot seem to overcome. When we consider something as goofy as a weasel defeating something so evil as a giant snake, perhaps we too can find hope that our struggles and temptations will also truly be defeated. The sins that we repeat in our lives and want to rid ourselves of, in order to grow closer to God, can be overcome. As Paul says in Philippians 4:13, "I have the strength for everything through him who empowers me."

Another instance of mythical animals in the Bible is in the book of Job 40:15–32. We are introduced to Behemoth and Leviathan.

> Look at Behemoth, whom I made along with you, who feeds on grass like an ox. See the strength in his loins, the power in the sinews of his belly. He carries his tail like a cedar; the sinews of his thighs are like cables. His bones are like tubes of bronze; his limbs are like iron rods. He is the first of God's ways, only his maker can approach him with a sword. For the mountains bring him produce, and all wild animals make sport there. Under lotus trees he lies, in coverts of the reedy swamp. The lotus trees cover him with their shade; all about him are the poplars in the wadi. If the river grows violent, he is not disturbed; he is tranquil though the Jordan surges about his mouth. Who can capture him by his eyes, or pierce his nose with a trap? Can you lead Leviathan about with a hook, or tie down his tongue with a rope? Can you put a ring into his nose, or pierce through his cheek with a gaff? Will he then plead with you, time after time, or address you with tender words? Will he make a covenant with you that you may have him as a slave forever? Can you play with him, as with a bird? Can you tie him up for your little girls? Will the traders bargain for him? Will the merchants divide him up? Can you fill his hide with barbs, or his head with fish

spears? Once you but lay a hand upon him, no need
to recall any other conflict!

Job is actually arguing with God, and there is a dialogue
going on between the two. God is speaking to Job about the
animals Behemoth and Leviathan. Some scholars conjecture that
Behemoth is describing a hippopotamus and that Leviathan was a
crocodile. Others conjecture that they are both monsters of chaos
that only God can control.[42] Theologian Michael D. Guinan,
OFM, goes a step further than this and suggests that the two beasts
are symbolic of Job. Guinan says, "the two beasts are meant as
symbols, even caricatures, of Job himself, who thrashes and struts
about saying, 'Everything is going back to chaos!'"[43]

Whatever is the true meaning of these creatures, their physical
attributes are positively terrifying and powerful. What strikes me
most is that when God mentions Behemoth in 40:15, "Look at
Behemoth, whom I made along with you," God mentions Job and
Behemoth as a creation. In Genesis 1:31, God looks out upon
his creation, "and found it very good." Even creatures or people
that seem hard to understand or to love, like the creatures in Job,
have a purpose in the story of creation. That man or woman at
work who drives you positively crazy has a purpose in the story of
creation. God loves the people we see as monsters in our lives just
as he loves us. That is a difficult statement to digest sometimes, but
it points us to the Golden Rule found in Matthew 7:12, "Do to
others whatever you would have them do to you."

Mythical Animals in the Lives of Saints

Naming some of the following animals as mythical may make
some people angry, like the Bigfoot believers who were upset with

me, as I mentioned earlier. Another set of believers I may offend, now, are believers in the Loch Ness Monster. We may be tempted to call folks crazy for believing in such a tale, but they have history and a saint on their side.

For those unfamiliar with the Loch Ness Monster, it is said to be a creature that lives in a giant lake called Loch Ness, in the Scottish Highlands. Sightings of the monster have gone back as many as 1500 years, and the first reported written sightings come to us from the legends of St. Columba.

In the year 565, St. Columba is said to have been walking near the River Ness, which flows out of Loch Ness, when he happened upon a group of men who were burying a man who was attacked and killed by a gigantic "water monster." Upon seeing that the beast was about to attack and kill another man, Columba is said to have made the sign of the cross in front of the monster and commanded it in the name of the Lord, "Do not touch the man! Leave at once!" Nessie, the nickname often given to the mythical creature, then departed and has become a tourist attraction ever since.[44]

Don't roll your eyes too much. Nessie and St. Columba can communicate some spiritual truths about the power of God over even gigantic "water monsters." In the face of the unknown, many of us flee or run in fear. The sight of an unknown, ferocious water monster probably filled Columba's heart with great fear and trepidation. He had faith that God's power could overcome even the most frightful things in life, and God acted through this faith, banishing Nessie to the depths through the sign of the cross. When we are encountering fear and uncertainty in our lives, this story can be a reminder that the cross of Christ has banished all evil to the depths of darkness, echoing the words of Psalm 23:4 in our heart and soul: "Even though I walk through the valley of the shadow of death, I will fear no evil, for you are with me."

Another great legend in the Catholic Church involving a mythical animal is the story of St. George and the Dragon. St. George was an imperial guard in the third-century Roman army of Diocletian, one of the worst persecutors of Christians in the history of the church. George was eventually martyred by the very emperor he served, but before that fateful day, he had a dragon to battle.

Near a spring in what is considered modern-day Libya, a dragon is said to have built a nest near where people would gather water for their daily chores. The people would offer the dragon sheep and even maidens to eat until one day, they ran out of maidens and sheep, and the princess was the only lady left to sacrifice. But before the princess could be fed to the dragon, it is said that St. George appeared before the beast, made the sign of the cross, and killed it. Witnessing this miraculous event, the local people then converted to Christianity.[45]

Minus the feeding of the local maidens to the dragon, this story has everything a fairy tale needs. A fearless soldier rides into battle to save the life of a princess while onlookers look on and believe in the power of God and convert to Christianity. The story of St. George and the dragon for me is a story of the people's conversion. The people were obviously in dire need of help as they were giving their own daughters to feed a ravenous beast. Like any stray animal, though, once you feed it, it will come back again and again. Witnessing this noble soldier ride in on horseback and stand toe to toe with the cause of the heartache and suffering must have filled them all with awe. What gave George such power to conquer such a mighty beast? The power of the cross. The hopes and fears of all the people were lifted when George defeated the dragon. Hope kindled a faith and love within them that burned brightly and longed for more. God was able to turn even this awful situation around to bring people closer to him. There is no dragon or beast that can stand against the power of the cross.

Catholic art throughout the ages is also resplendent with mythical animals. The gargoyle is a creature that has stood through the ages atop Gothic cathedrals and churches as a way to keep water from gathering on rooftops. It has also been used as a teaching tool to the Catholic faithful. Daniel Esparaza, in the article titled, "How Gargoyles Save Souls...and Ceilings," says that these frightening stone creatures "reinforce the notion that evil remains *outside* the church, metaphorically and literally, and that evil flees from the holy places: 'Upon this rock I will build my church, and all the powers of hell will not conquer it.' It was a way to graphically represent what is written in Scripture, in times when there were few who could read and write."[46]

I have always found gargoyles ugly and terrifying creatures. If they are a representation of some of the evil that is found in hell, then I do not want to go there. Fear of hell is not the main reason to grow in a faith-filled relationship with Christ, but it certainly doesn't hurt to have a reminder from time to time that evil and the devil exist in the world, and that we need to check our relationship with God to see how we are living our lives. Having these creatures sit on the roofs of the most beautiful churches in the world reminds us to flee inside to the saving arms of Jesus and his Church.

Lastly, it is best to remember that the Bible is not written as a science book to help us understand scientific facts. Each book is written to reveal something deeper and more profound about God and the story of salvation and love of his people. These stories of mythical creatures in Scripture and throughout the lives of Catholic saints may defy our beliefs and the fossil records. Though proof of some of these animals may not technically exist, these animals, like all created things, can draw us closer to God.

FAT COWS

"Eat mor chikin"
—THE CHICK-FIL-A COWS

To be called a fat cow by another human being may seem like a horrendous insult to most people. I have lived my entire life around cattle and have heard many siblings, teenagers, and friends call one another a fat cow. In fact, I have probably called my brothers fat cows at one time or another. However, the more I contemplate the term, and taking my experience with cattle, I think we may be able to turn the phrase "fat cow" into a colossal compliment.

For starters, let us consider the temperament of most cows. Cows are very calm creatures that enjoy their days grazing peacefully in beautiful green pastures. As a young child growing up on a cattle farm in Arkansas, rarely did I witness a cow get angry and attack its owner. In fact, one of my favorite things in childhood was riding around the farm, not on a beautiful saddled horse, but on a giant, 1500-pound Holstein named Pet. Pet possessed the gentleness of a saint. My father would pick up my four-year old self and place me atop Pet's massive black and white back. We did not gallop at amazing speeds, but we took more of a leisurely stroll around the feedlot. Still, in my young mind, Pet was a horse in the old West, galloping away from the sheriff and his deputies after we had just robbed a bank. Never did anger or fear force the heart of this bovine to become unsettled and toss me off. She calmly accepted my presence and kindly endured my childhood.

Researchers have found that if you name a cow, and care for it, that cow will produce five hundred more pints of milk a year than an unnamed cow alone in a field.[47] This means that the cow is a social animal that is able to function at its best when loved. Who isn't? Cows also spend most of the day in large herds, enjoying one another's company as they wade in muddy ponds or lounge and nap together on a hot summer day beneath the shade of a giant oak tree.

Cows are also very good at caring for their calves. My father has often commented that mother cows will babysit for one another when one of the mothers is off away from the herd. I am not sure if this is a scientific fact or not, but I consider my father a "Cattle Whisperer," so his observation in this instance probably has some shred of fact.

But what about a cow's physical traits and abilities? Scientific studies have concluded that a cow is able to smell an odor up to six miles away while being able to see up to 300 degrees around their entire body, with the only two visual blind spots being right in front and directly behind them. Scientists have also learned that cows moo with accents. "After a group of dairy farmers noticed their cows had different moos, language specialists determined that, 'In small populations such as herds you would encounter identifiable dialectical variations which are most affected by the immediate peer group.'"[48] In layperson's terms, cows that live in one pasture may moo differently from cows in a different pasture, just as we humans in different parts of the world speak with different accents.

Cows are also fat. A skinny cow is a sick cow. Cows are designed by God to be bigger so they can produce milk, stay warm, and be a source of food for us. No one wants a skinny cow. So, to be a cow, and to be fat, is a good thing.

With the above information, it seems like calling someone a fat cow is quite the compliment. Basically, they are saying you are a nice, caring person with a calm attitude, who loves to be around others; you can see and smell really well, and you are made as God intended you to be. If that is what it means to be called a fat cow, then we should all be fat cows.

Cows in the Bible

Cows in Sacred Scripture have historically stood for patience, strength, sacrifice, and fortitude.[49] In the Old Testament book of Genesis chapter 41:1–4, the Egyptian Pharaoh has a dream about fat cows being devoured by skinny cows. The verses say, "After a lapse of two years, Pharaoh had a dream. He was standing by the Nile, when up out of the Nile came seven cows, fine-looking and fat; they grazed in the reed grass. Behind them seven other cows, poor-looking and gaunt, came up out of the Nile; and standing on the bank of the Nile beside the others, the poor-looking, gaunt cows devoured the seven fine-looking, fat cows. Then Pharaoh woke up."

Even though the knowledge of the agricultural sciences of ancient Egypt were probably not up to our standards today, it is safe to assume the Egyptians know that cows do not eat other cows, and therefore this dream is a particularly disturbing one to Pharaoh. He calls in his magicians and sages for an interpretation, but none of them are able to explain it. Then, the chief cupbearer remembers a Hebrew boy named Joseph, who is able to correctly interpret dreams. Joseph interprets the dream, telling Pharaoh in Genesis 41:25–27: "Pharaoh's dreams have the same meaning. God has made known to Pharaoh what he is about to do. The seven healthy cows are seven years, and the seven healthy ears are seven years—the same in each dream. The seven thin, bad cows that came up after them are seven years, as are the seven thin ears scorched by the east wind; they are seven years of famine."

In these passages, the cattle appear only in a dream. However, their physical state and their representation of seven years of famine and seven years of health represent the virtue of fortitude and patience for the Egyptians. Bible commentator Pauline Viviano comments that "Joseph follows his interpretation with practical advice, which Pharaoh immediately accepts."[50] Pharaoh knows that Egypt is in for a hard time in the future, and if his people do not immediately act and prepare to endure the harsh famine, they will not survive. Surviving this catastrophe will require all of the cows' symbolic representation of patience, strength, sacrifice, and fortitude.

Also, because Joseph is able to accurately interpret Pharaoh's dream about the upcoming famine, Joseph finds favor with Pharaoh, and Pharaoh places him in charge of all of Egypt. Because of this position, Joseph is later able to save his family from starvation and be united with them after many years apart.

All of these great blessings came about in Joseph's life because he was able to tell Pharaoh what his cow-eating-cow dream meant. This story is another reminder to us that God works in mysterious ways, and just because we do not see an answer to our prayers in a current situation, that does not mean there is not one on the horizon.

There are many cows in Scripture.

In Exodus chapter 32, an image of a cow plays a role that many of us are already very familiar with. Moses has led the

Israelites out of slavery in Egypt and is up on top of Mount
Sinai speaking with the Lord. Moses stays on the mountain for a
very long time with God. In fact, Moses is gone so long, that the
Israelites become worried that something has happened to him.
They come to a decision that they should make a god of their
own that will not leave them like Moses and God have seemingly
done. To do this, they gather gold and jewelry from one another
and have Aaron, Moses's brother, construct for them a false god,
a golden calf. The Israelites then begin to worship the calf by
sacrificing offerings to it, drinking, eating, and reveling.

From the top of the mountain, God tells Moses what the
Israelites are doing down below, and that he is thinking of wiping
them off the face of the earth in his anger. Moses pleads with
God to spare them by reminding God of the covenant he made
with Abraham. God remembers the covenant and spares Israel.
Moses comes off the mountain with the Ten Commandments in
hand and then destroys the golden calf.

When reading this story, I often wonder why the Israelites built
a golden calf instead of a golden turtle or a golden elephant?
Most of the early church fathers and some biblical scholars today
believe that the Israelites borrowed the worship of golden calves
from the ancient Egyptians. However, there are others who think
because the Israelites were an agricultural people, they saw the
bull as a symbol of strength and vitality and thus adopted the
animal for that reason.[51] The story of the golden calf, if looked at
from a perspective other than idolatry, can also be read in a way
that affirms the symbolism of cows throughout salvation history
as a symbol of patience and strength.

It is a difficult thing to be patient and wait on the Lord. The
Israelites grew impatient and forgot Moses's words from earlier
in Exodus 14:14, "The LORD will fight for you; you have only to

keep still." These same words apply to us today. We often want to force God's hand and have him act in some incredible way in our lives. When we do not receive what we want from God exactly how we want it, we become like the Israelites and try to take matters into our own hands. We begin to build our own golden calves to help us get what we desire. The golden calf is very much a false god in the biblical story, but it can be used as a learning opportunity for us to remember that we have a God of infinite love who wants our faith to strengthen through trustful patience.

In the New Testament, a cow being sacrificed is actually at the center of a great celebration. Luke chapter 15 gives us the familiar story of the Prodigal Son. In the story, a son asks his father for his inheritance and goes off and squanders it on a life of drunkenness and pleasure. A severe famine hits the country and the son loses everything. He becomes so destitute that he dreams of returning home to be, not his father's son, but a hired worker who has a roof over his head and food on the table. However, while he is still a long way off from home, the son finds that his father is outside waiting for his return. The father sees the son and runs out to meet him, embracing him with love. The son tries to ask forgiveness, but the father will have none of that and is just thankful to have him home. He calls for a celebration! His son who was once very lost has now been found, and to celebrate, they slaughter the fatted calf.

Biblical scholar Jerome Kodell, OSB, says this about the story of the prodigal son: "A parable this rich blossoms out with new meaning for each reader, and at each reading."[52] As I reflect on the calf in what is one of Jesus's most famous parables, I cannot help seeing an image of Jesus. Jesus was slaughtered so that we would be able to celebrate an eternal feast with him in heaven. Similarly, the calf was slaughtered so that the father's mercy for his prodigal son could be celebrated by all. In both instances, innocence, sacrifice, and celebration are present. The calf may play only a small part, but it still stands true to the cow's representation of sacrifice throughout Scripture. Through this sacrifice comes mercy, and through mercy comes a celebration for all those who ask God the Father.

Cows in the Lives of Saints, Past and Present

Cows have also played an important role both physically and symbolically in the lives of saints and future saints.

One of the worst acts of nickname bullying in the history of the church is related to a cow. St. Thomas Aquinas, a thirteenth-century Italian Dominican priest, was one of the most brilliant minds our planet has ever known. His theological works thunder through the ages of the faith even to this day. However, he was a bit on the chubby side according to some sources, and was slow to speak. So his buddies in school nicknamed him "Dumb Ox."[53] For those who do not know, an ox is a type of cow, so basically, they were calling him a dumb, fat cow. If you recall, I am working hard to have the phrase "fat cow" changed to a compliment, so if that ever happens, I hope to get a high five from St. Thomas in heaven.

G. K. Chesterton, in his book *Saint Thomas Aquinas: The Dumb Ox*, had this to say about the mean nickname: "[St. Albert the Great knew] that the dunce is not always a dunce . . . his famous cry and prophecy [about Thomas] – 'You can call him a Dumb Ox; I tell you this Dumb Ox shall bellow so loud that his bellowings will fill the world.' "[54]

Like some of the examples of cows in Scripture, St. Thomas and his nickname show us the virtue of fortitude. Thomas, though made fun of and bullied, could have closed himself off to the world in fear because of the chiding of his childhood mates. He pressed on, demonstrating the symbolic fortitude of the cow, and overcame the voices mocking him. It takes strength to persevere and do what God asks of us when we are made fun of or ridiculed for our beliefs, but, like the Dumb Ox, we all must press on.

Turning from the ridiculed to the miraculous, the fifth-century Irish saint Brigid of Kildare was a woman who worked many miracles that involved animals. One of these had to do with a cow that had already been milked dry. It is said that St. Brigid touched the cow and miraculously the cow was able to produce milk ten times the normal amount a cow would produce.[55]

To put this in perspective, the average Holstein cow today produces about nine gallons of milk a day. St. Brigid's cow must have produced around an amazing ninety gallons of milk in one day!

This story of miraculous milk is for me a reminder of the strength of my family. My father grew up on a dairy farm and would rise every morning with my grandfather at three or four in the morning to milk cattle before going off to school. Even though his cows did not produce ten times as much milk as a normal cow, like St. Brigid's, his cows did instill in him a strength of work ethic to provide for his family. He might have slept in a little later if he'd had one of Brigid's cows, but he would also not be the man he is today if he had.

Finally, in researching cows in the history of our church, I also came across a Blessing for Diseased Cattle. It is a rather old prayer, and some of the language can seem a tad archaic to us today, but it is a blessing that could apply not just for a cow, but I think any animal. It also goes to show that if you need to pray about anything at all, God is ready to listen.

O Lord, deal not with us according to our sins, nor
reward us according to our iniquities. Thou healest

men and beasts, for Thy mercy is great. Thou openest Thy hand, and fillest with blessing every living creature.

O God, who hast decreed that the dumb animals should help man in his labors, we humbly pray Thee, do not permit these animals to perish, because without them man cannot support and nourish himself.

We call upon Thy mercy, O Lord, without ceasing grant that these animals, afflicted with grievous disease, may be restored to health in Thy name and by the power of Thy blessing. May all the power of the devil be driven from them so that they will languish no more. Be Thou, O Lord, the protector of their lives and the healer of their ailments.

Turn away from us, O Lord, we beseech Thee, the scourges of Thy punishment and drive off this disease that attacks these animals, as Thou punishest those who wander from Thy paths, but givest Thy grace when they have amended their lives. Through Christ our Lord. Amen.[56]

This prayer called to mind a time when a cow once helped me grow closer to God. One cold, rainy afternoon during wintertime, I was out in a pasture near my home feeding my father's cattle. If you have never had the joy of feeding a herd of cows a bucket of feed, let me explain how this can become a potentially dangerous situation.

A five-gallon bucket of feed is poured down a long, concrete trough that the cattle gather around to eat. While this happens, cows the size of small cars jump up and down all around you like excited children at Chuck E. Cheese, waiting for their turn to graze at the table. One of these cows was so excited that she backed up and crunched down atop my foot. In a very holy gesture of prayer, I dropped into the mud on my knees. I could hardly breathe. The pain was so intense that no sound escaped my mouth. I looked up to the heavens, and though I was physically unable to say a prayer with my voice, I know that God heard the one being prayed in my heart. "Dear Lord, please make this pain stop!" Days later my foot finally stopped hurting, and thankfully nothing was broken. You may not see this as a miraculous event, but I am happy that I was not injured worse than what I endured and can thank God to this day that I was not.

I would like to make one final case for changing the "fat cow" insult into a compliment. We have seen how cows can be a symbol for patience, strength, fortitude, and sacrifice in the Bible and in the lives of saints. Experiences with them can range from dreams, statues, injuries, and even prayers that help us grow in virtue.

Cow symbolism can even be found in contemporary music, drawing upon those virtues found in Scripture and the lives of saints that help us grow closer to God. Singer and songwriter Jimmy Buffett plays his smash hit "Cheeseburger in Paradise" at almost every single concert. It is about wanting to eat a cheeseburger on a beautiful tropical island where cows are particularly hard to find. When a cheeseburger is finally found to eat on one of these islands, it is a paradise of culinary delight. This song teaches us that even when we find ourselves stuck in heaven on earth, a tropical island in the middle of nowhere, we are still patiently waiting, hoping, and searching for a fat cow to share it with. I cannot think of too many other animals or people that would be honored with that great compliment.

BEHOLD, THE LAMB

"Behold, the Lamb of God,
who takes away the sin of the world."
—JOHN 1:29

or five minutes on an "L" train in Chicago, I witnessed what world peace would truly look like. I observed people of all races, cultures, creeds, and backgrounds coming together as one to live in happiness and harmony together. In short, I witnessed a glimpse of heaven, the reason a spotless lamb was slaughtered for us all.

What does world peace and a glimpse of heaven look like, you might be wondering? To answer you rather bluntly, it looks just like my bachelor party.

On a lovely day in June, my friends and I boarded a plane to travel to one of the places I love going to most in all of the world: Wrigley Field. I love the Chicago Cubs. I was first enamored by listening to the rambling voice of Harry Caray talk about almost everything but the baseball game going on right in front of him during the WGN baseball broadcasts I watched after school as a teenager. That love was forever solidified with a visit to Wrigley

Field when I was sixteen. I sat in the outfield bleachers as one of the world-famous Bleacher Bums. Therefore, my friends thought that this would be the best place to take me to celebrate the end of my life as a single man and my entrance into the life of wedded bliss.

As I mentioned, world peace was not experienced on the baseball field, but on the Chicago "L" train after the game. For those of you unfamiliar with Chicago, "L" is short for "elevated," and it's the rapid transit system that services the city and its surrounding suburbs and makes traveling to and from Wrigley Field very efficient.

The Cubs won the game, and we boarded the train at the Addison stop behind Wrigley to take us back to our hotel. Perhaps you've heard that many people at Major League baseball games sometimes partake of an alcoholic beverage or ten at the ballpark. Many of the thirty or more people that boarded our train that day had obviously consumed copious amounts of libations.

Three minutes into the ride, we began to hear a commotion at the back of the train. Now, a commotion in a public place can bring feelings of fear and panic. However, our fears were alleviated when we began hearing people cheering and counting "one, two, three, four. . . ." My friends and I looked back to see a slightly inebriated young man doing pull-ups on the handrail of the train, while the people around him were counting how many he did. After ten, he stopped, and everyone quit counting and cheered.

Not wanting to be outdone by the back of the train, I suggested to my friend Ben that he could possibly beat ten. Ben grabbed the rail above him and began a pull-up session Hercules would have found impressive, easily beating the ten of the man at the back of the train. While Ben did these pull-ups, people around him became caught up in the drama and began counting and encouraging him on.

Once Ben was finished with his set, I assumed the contest would be over, but the guys at the back were not to be underestimated or beaten so easily. They started pull-ups once again to beat Ben, and everyone on the train, front, middle, and back were cheering them on. There were folks of all different races, creeds, and backgrounds on the train that day, and for a brief moment, all of them were smiling and encouraging their fellow man in his feat of strength. I looked around and saw joy on every face.

Many people were shocked that something like this was even happening. I caught a glimpse of heaven that day, when the world was at peace and everyone was filled with joy. Heaven will be infinitely greater than that experience, and it will all be because of the spotless lamb that was slain for our sins.

Lambs in the Bible

In a mysterious way, God chose the lamb, sheep, and ram (three different forms of the same animal) to play an amazing part in salvation history, both physically and symbolically. This beautiful and peaceful animal has always been a prophetic symbol of the Son of God, Jesus, who saves us from our sins.

In the book of Genesis 22:1–19, God calls Abraham to the land of Moriah to offer up his beloved son Isaac as a sacrifice. Isaac, however, is oblivious to the fact that he is about to be sacrificed, thinking that the sacrifice to God will be the usual sheep or ram. In this circumstance, ignorance is bliss for Isaac. He and his father Abraham set off to the appointed land to follow God's command. When they arrive at the place of sacrifice, Isaac becomes a bit confused because his father has wood but no sheep for the offering. In what must be one of the most traumatic moments of his beloved son's life, Abraham binds Isaac so he is unable to move. He then places Isaac on the altar in an act of absolute obedience to God and is about to slaughter him when God suddenly commands Abraham to stop and not slay the boy. God recognizes Abraham's faithfulness to him and his command and thus spares Isaac's life.

In order to still be obedient to God's command to offer a sacrifice, Abraham comes across a ram with its horns stuck in a thicket. He takes it and offers it as a sacrifice instead of his son. In this way, the ram that takes the place of a beloved son becomes the foreshadowing of the only begotten son of God, offered as a spotless sacrifice instead for our sins. Commentators in the *Ignatius Catholic Study Bible* point out how the early Fathers of the Church linked the significance and foreshadowing of the ram being caught in a thicket with Jesus being crowned with thorns at the Crucifixion.[57] In their own way, both wore a crown of thorns on their way to death in place of someone else.

As with Abraham in Genesis, the Israelites would once again let a lamb or sheep take the place of their lives as a sacrifice. In the book of Exodus, the Israelites are held under the yoke of slavery by the Egyptians. God has already sent nine plagues to the Egyptians so that they would free his covenant people. Pharaoh's heart was hardened after each plague, and he would not release the Israelites from slavery. In the last plague God inflicted upon the Egyptians, the Angel of the Lord was to come at night and kill every firstborn in Egypt, the Israelites included. In order for the Angel of Death to pass over the Israelite homes, a lamb would once again prove instrumental in saving the lives of God's beloved.

Exodus 12:5–11 describes how a one-year-old unblemished lamb must be slaughtered, breaking no bones, and eaten by an Israelite family. The lamb's blood must then be smeared on the door lintels so that the Angel of Death could identify God's people and pass over them. The blood of the lamb took the place of the Israelites' firstborn, and as with Isaac, was their salvation.

Scripture scholar George Leo Haydock comments how the lamb at the Passover meal is also a foreshadowing of Jesus in our Eucharistic meal. "The paschal lamb prefigured Jesus Christ, who has redeemed us by his death, being holy, set apart, and condescending to feed us with his sacred person, in the blessed Eucharist. Here we eat the lamb without breaking a bone, though we take the whole victim. To fulfill this figure, Christ substituted his own body, and, making his apostles priests, ordered them to continue this sacrifice for ever."[58]

In the New Testament, the slaughtering of an unblemished lamb is finally replaced by the slaughtering of the true unblemished, sinless lamb, Jesus. In John 1:29, John the Baptist is baptizing people in the Jordan River when he catches sight of Jesus coming towards him. He cries out, "Behold, the Lamb of God, who takes away the sin of the world." Paragraph 608 of the *Catechism of the Catholic Church* points out the importance of John the Baptist's proclamation of Jesus as the Lamb of God:

> After agreeing to baptize him along with the sinners, John the Baptist looked at Jesus and pointed him out as the "Lamb of God, who takes away the sin of the world." By doing so, he reveals that Jesus is at the same time the suffering Servant who silently allows himself to be led to the slaughter and who bears the sin of the multitudes, and also the Paschal Lamb, the symbol of Israel's redemption at the first Passover. Christ's whole life expresses his mission: "to serve, and to give his life as a ransom for many."[59]

Free of sin, he is slaughtered so that we may be saved from death, as were the Israelites and Isaac, and now all of salvation history has been redeemed by the blood of the lamb.

Lambs in the Lives of Saints

The lives of Catholic saints are also resplendent with stories of sheep bringing people closer to Christ and helping them grow in their spiritual lives. In fact, I have almost decided that if you are a shepherd and are very holy, there is a possibility that you will have a Marian apparition, become a saint, or go into heavenly ecstasies on a regular basis.

There have been times throughout history when Mary has chosen to reveal herself supernaturally. Some of these occurred in obscure areas of the world to shepherds tending sheep. If you are a skeptic of these events, let us state the official Catholic belief on approved Marian apparitions: "According to the doctrine of the Catholic Church, the era of public revelation ended with the death of the last living Apostle. A Marian apparition, if deemed genuine by Church authority, is treated as private revelation that may emphasize some facet of the received public revelation for a specific purpose, but it can never add anything new to the deposit of faith. The Church will confirm an apparition as worthy of belief, but belief is never required by divine faith."[60]

On August 21, 1878, fifteen people in Knock, Ireland, witnessed an apparition of Mary, St. Joseph, and St. John the Evangelist near a lamb and a cross that sat on top of an altar near the wall of their parish church. The apparition lasted two hours, and while it went on, the people recited the Rosary together. The witnesses ranged from five to seventy-four years old. One of the interesting aspects of this apparition, when compared to other approved Marian apparitions of the Church, is the presence of the lamb. Witnesses to the apparition attested that the lamb was staring at Mary and seemed to be radiating light as light shone forth from its body. Also, because the lamb sat atop the altar, it is thought to be symbolic of Jesus being the spotless lamb who was slain for our sins.[61]

My friend Patrick and I visited Knock in 2007. It was a beautiful, out-of-the-way place in Ireland that radiated holiness just like the lamb in the apparition that radiated light for all to see. The place where the apparition happened now has white statues in place of all of the figures that appeared that evening in the way and in the formation in which they appeared. The lamb atop the altar surely is facing in the direction of the Blessed Mother Mary, while St. John the Evangelist holds open a book of the Gospels.

This scene also calls to mind a scene from the Crucifixion. In John 19:26–27, as Jesus hangs dying, nailed to a cross, he fixes his gaze upon his mother and then upon John the Evangelist, who later wrote, "When Jesus saw his mother and the disciple there whom he loved, he said to his mother, 'Woman, behold, your son.' Then he said to the disciple, 'Behold, your mother.' And from that hour the disciple took her into his home."

Looking at the statues at the Knock shrine, we can almost see the story of salvation unfold before our eyes, while also being taught how to grow closer to God. The lamb sitting atop the altar at Knock is Jesus, who was slain for our sins, and who is the one we receive in the Eucharist during Mass. The lamb's intense gaze upon Mary introduces us to our mother and reminds us of her words from John 2:5 at the wedding at Cana, when she tells the servers to "Do whatever he tells you." Next to Mary at Knock stands John the Evangelist, who holds the Gospels out for all to see and invites us to consume the story of this lamb who redeems the world. This calls to mind the words of St. Jerome, "Ignorance of the Scriptures is ignorance of Christ."[62]

Another Marian apparition is the one that took place in Fatima, Portugal, in 1917. In this apparition, an angel first appeared to three children, Lucia, Francisco, and Jacinta, while they were in a field tending their sheep. The shepherd children were then visited by Mary six other times between May 13, 1917, and October 13, 1917.

One of the great messages of Fatima was to pray for the conversion of sinners every day, and to renew devotion to the praying of the Rosary. These three humble shepherds, through these prayers and devotions, have shepherded many twentieth- and twenty-first-century saints closer to the Good Shepherd, Jesus, reminding us that the only true way to love one another is as a shepherd loves his sheep. As Jesus says in the Gospel:

> Amen, amen, I say to you, whoever does not enter a sheepfold through the gate but climbs over elsewhere is a thief and a robber. But whoever enters through the gate is the shepherd of the sheep. The gatekeeper opens it for him, and the sheep hear his voice, as he calls his own sheep by name and leads them out. When he has driven out all his own, he walks ahead of them, and the sheep follow him, because they recognize his voice. But they will not follow a stranger; they will run away from him, because they do not recognize the voice of strangers. (John 10:1–5)

Although Jesus used this figure of speech, they did not realize what he was trying to tell them. So Jesus said again,

> Amen, amen, I say to you, I am the gate for the sheep. All who came [before me] are thieves and robbers,

but the sheep did not listen to them. I am the gate. Whoever enters through me will be saved, and will come in and go out and find pasture. A thief comes only to steal and slaughter and destroy; I came so that they might have life and have it more abundantly. I am the good shepherd. A good shepherd lays down his life for the sheep. (John 10:7–11)

A sixteenth-century figure, St. Germaine Cousin, spent long days in the field tending sheep. However, every day, she would leave her sheep in the care of God to attend daily Mass, and every day her sheep were kept safe. She was also forced at one point in her life to live in a barn, with the only warmth coming from the sheep that also slept there. At night she would sleep near the sheep so that she was able to survive the cold.[63]

St. Clement of Rome, the fourth pope, was once arrested during the Christian persecutions in first-century Rome and sent to work at a marble quarry with some of his fellow Christian convicts. There was no water to be found anywhere near the quarry. In fact, the closest water was many miles away, and many of the Christians suffered greatly at the hard labor and lack of water. One day Clement saw a lamb scraping at the soil with one of its feet, and he took this as a sign that water was located in that position. He dug and found a spring, now making water easily accessible to those in the quarries.[64]

Is it an accident that we see a sheep or lamb taking the role of physical lifesaver? Sheep kept St. Germaine from freezing to death while she slept in a cold barn, and a lamb helped quench the thirst of many persecuted Christians in the first century. These two instances show that though Jesus was the lamb who was killed for all, God still uses his beautiful, wooly creatures to help us survive physically today.

Sheep and lambs have played an integral part in salvation history, especially as symbols of sacrifice and forgiveness. However, there is one last personal tidbit of information I would like to add about how lambs have affected my faith.

My wife loves stuffed animals. She has fifteen around her while she is sleeping at all times. Two of these we call the "Bed Lambs." The story goes that when we were dating, I found and bought her two of the cutest stuffed lambs in the history of the world; we named them Lambie and Queso. They have been hanging out with her and on the bed ever since. I highly recommend that you get a pair of "Bed Lambs" for your home as well, because they help serve as a reminder of all the things the lamb has done for our faith. They also bring to my mind memories of the ultimate price that was paid for my salvation, and that is a beautiful reminder to me of the life that will be in the world to come.

CAT-HOLIC

"The smallest feline is a masterpiece."
—LEONARDO DA VINCI

Cats are my jam. I love cats. I have two and would have them all if my wife would let me. I am a crazy cat lady in training although I am not a lady nor completely crazy, yet. Bring me your fluffs! The Tabbys, Siamese, Calicos, Russian Blues, Tuxedos, Norwegians, Maine Coons, Tortoiseshells, strays, one-eyed, one-whiskered, one-pawed, hypoallergenic hairless ones—I will pet them all. I am both a Catholic and a Cat-holic and proud of it.

At what point in my life did I realize I was a certified, crazy cat person? I believe I was about twenty-five years old and had just taken my new kitten, Ana, to the veterinarian to be spayed. I was so worried about her being by herself all alone in an unknown place for twenty-four hours that I called the veterinarian and asked if I could take her home early. He said that I could that afternoon, and so I drove over to the clinic and picked her up. She was still groggy most of the night from the anesthesia, and I sat with her in my bathroom watching all night to make sure she was safe, cared for, and not alone. That is the moment that I knew I had gone cat crazy.

Cats truly are amazing creatures, and there are some scientific facts as to why I may feel the way I do about them. Scientists say that playing with a cat between fifteen and thirty minutes a day can calm people's nerves and put them in a good mood. Your body's production of the chemical serotonin goes up and the production of cortisol goes down. Serotonin is a chemical that boosts happy feelings, while cortisol is a chemical that boosts stress levels. In fact, in a twenty-year study, scientists found that people who own a cat are 40 percent less likely to die of a heart attack.[65] I think that means that if I owned four cats, I would be 160 percent less likely to die of a heart attack, and that if I owned all the cats, it would be very difficult for me to die at all. I am not sure that my math or my reasoning are correct, but I have a good feeling about this.

Some other amazing facts about cats that promote health for their owners is that they are capable of purring at a vibration between 25 to 150 Hertz, which is the same frequency used for bone and muscle repair in the human body. Who needs healthcare, right? It is very clear from these scientific facts that people just need to open up rooms full of purring and loving cats to heal them of their most serious ailments.[66]

I am not alone in my admiration and love of the cat. Many famous and wonderful people before me have also been "cat happy." Mary Todd Lincoln was once asked what her husband Abraham Lincoln's hobby was, and she replied "cats."[67] Pope St. John Paul II also loved and owned cats. In 1894, Thomas Edison recorded the first ever cat video, now popular on social media and YouTube. The video, titled "The Boxing Cats," featured two cats in a tiny boxing ring, wearing tiny cat-sized boxing gloves and boxing each other. I am not exactly sure of the Rotten Tomatoes score on this film, but I bet it was a knockout for 1894.

If you were to take a look at my wife's cell phone camera roll, you would not find romantic pictures of her and me in exotic destinations looking lovingly into each other's eyes with a gorgeous sunset behind us. Instead, you would find photo after photo of our two indoor calicos in different places in the house with different camera filters, just sitting there staring oddly at her as she documents their lives on her phone. Thomas Edison may have been innovative with the cat video, but my wife is currently perfecting it.

My cats are truly a part of my family and hold a special place in my heart. They are beside me in good times and bad, in sickness and in health, just like my wife. They are a part of my family and have brought much joy to me. They have blessed my life in a positive way, and they have also had a noteworthy influence in Scripture and in the lives of the saints.

Cats in the Bible

In a not very shocking turn of events, I have found that Orange Tabby cats are not mentioned once in the Bible. In fact, the only time that a word meaning something resembling a simple house cat comes up in Scripture is in the book of Baruch 6:21: "Bats and swallows alight on their bodies and heads—any bird, and cats as well." So, for our study of cats, we will pivot to their illustrious relative, the lion.

Though the lion is no longer found around Israel and Palestine and the surrounding countries, during the time of the Old Testament they were prevalent. Bible scholars throughout history have concluded that in Scripture, the lion is known "as the classical symbol of strength, power, courage, dignity, ferocity."[68] When we meet with lions in the Bible, their strength and power is used to show just how much stronger God is than what we consider to be powerful and strong in this world.

In the Book of Judges 14:5–6, Samson literally tears a lion into pieces. "So Samson went down to Timnah with his father and mother. When he turned aside to the vineyards of Timnah, a young lion came roaring out toward him. But the spirit of the LORD rushed upon Samson, and he tore the lion apart barehanded, as one tears a young goat."

In *The Collegeville Bible Commentary*, John A. Grindel, CM, comments, "It is the spirit of the Lord that gives Samson the strength to deal so easily with the lion."[69] No man should be able to kill a lion barehanded, much less tear one to pieces. Samson and the lion show us that though a lion's strength is of this world, God created the lion and is able to overcome its power.

For all of us who struggle trying to conquer certain sins in our life, the story of Samson ripping apart an animal as powerful as a lion should give us hope. Yes, a hope that through God's power and mercy, we may overcome the evil effects of sin. If God can give a man the strength to tear a lion apart, he can empower you to overcome your vices and draw closer to his love. If you fall, do not give up hope; God is beside you, helping you back up to try again, so that through patient endurance, faith, and mercy, you may overcome the devil, who "is prowling around like a roaring lion looking for [someone] to devour" (1 Pet. 5:8).

In the first book of Samuel, we see how the strength of a lion is once again overcome by the power of God through the figure of King David. As David is about to engage in battle with the Philistine Goliath, Saul tries to talk him out of fighting because of Goliath's great size and strength. David, though, has battled and conquered the strength of a lion because God delivered him.

> Then David told Saul: "Your servant used to tend
> his father's sheep, and whenever a lion or bear came
> to carry off a sheep from the flock, I would chase

after it, attack it, and snatch the prey from its mouth. If it attacked me, I would seize it by the throat, strike it, and kill it. Your servant has killed both a lion and a bear. This uncircumcised Philistine will be as one of them, because he has insulted the armies of the living God." David continued: "The same LORD who delivered me from the claws of the lion and the bear will deliver me from the hand of this Philistine." Saul answered David, "Go! the LORD will be with you." (1 Sam. 17:34–37)

Lions are extremely large and powerful creatures. From their head to the start of their tail they are five to eight feet long and weigh 300 to 400 pounds. Plus, they are programmed with catlike quickness and stalking abilities. David has faced one of the most ferocious predators that the world can throw at him, and so he does not fear Goliath. God has power over Goliath as he did over the lion, calling to mind the words David wrote in Psalm 27:1, "The LORD is my light and my salvation; whom should I fear? The LORD is my life's refuge; of whom should I be afraid?"

No chapter about cats would be complete without the story of Daniel in the Lion's Den found in the sixth chapter of the Book of Daniel. Daniel, along with many others, was appointed by King Darius of Persia to the high office of satrap. A satrap was a local governor of a certain province of ancient Persia.[70] Daniel was by far the best at his job, and the other satraps became jealous of his success and conspired to kill him. So in their cunning, they devised a law that said for thirty days no one could say a prayer or petition to anyone, human or divine, except King Darius. If they did, they were to be thrown into a den of lions.

The men who devised this plan found Daniel in his home praying to God. They knew they would; Daniel had a reputation as a person of prayer. The men ran and told the king that Daniel had broken the new law, and Daniel was thrown into a den of lions. The king told Daniel, "Your God, whom you serve so constantly, must save you" (Dan. 6:22). The next morning, Daniel was found safe and sound. He told King Darius that the Angel of the Lord protected him through the night and kept the lions' mouths closed.

This passage and story again demonstrate how God has power above and beyond what he has created. A lion has the tenth most powerful bite in the world, rated at 650 pounds per square inch.[71] In other words, if you are bitten by one, this is not a good thing! All night, the Angel of the Lord kept Daniel safe by closing the jaws of one of the most fearsome animals in the world. The Angel did not tire; he was sent by God, and God never tires of loving and protecting us.

As mentioned earlier, the fearsome and powerful might of the lion is used in the New Testament in 1 Peter 5:8–9 to symbolize the strength and terror the devil implores to destroy a soul. "Be sober and vigilant. Your opponent the devil is prowling around like a roaring lion looking for [someone] to devour. Resist him, steadfast in faith, knowing that your fellow believers throughout the world undergo the same sufferings." Jerome H. Neyrey, SJ, interprets these words as a call to faith in God. He says, "The 'God of all grace' wants us to be happy and he will vindicate us from suffering, just as he raised up his son, Jesus. Our God is loving, powerful, trustworthy, and faithful. And to him we give dominion forever and ever."[72] We have no reason to fear the strength of the devil. God has dominion over him just as he does the strength of the lion. When we remain faithful to God, no power can overcome us, and we can live our faith fearlessly.

Cats in the Lives of Saints

Though domesticated cats are uncommon in Scripture, they are common in the lives of saints, and their presence throughout the lives of these holy men and women of the Church continues to show that God is in control of the created world around us.

For starters, there is a rather interesting story with cats and a saint who was bedridden because of a disease. Blessed Maria Bagnesi was a very holy sixteenth-century Dominican tertiary. Her reputation spread far and wide, and people came to her room to seek her counsel and prayers. It is also said that cats had a special love for her. They would come and stay with her in her room, sleep on her bed, guard her pet bird, and sometimes even bring her food to eat.[73]

A story by Chuck Raasch of *USA Today* published in 2013 says, "Cats that live in the wild or indoor pets allowed to roam outdoors kill from 1.4 billion to as many as 3.7 billion birds in the continental U.S. each year."[74] Bl. Maria Bagnesi's cats guarded her pet bird, throwing the entire predator versus prey matchup upside down. In this instance, God shows not only his power over his creation, but that his creation can truly embody the words of Romans 12:18: "Live at peace with all."

St. Gertrude of Nivelles was a seventh-century Benedictine saint who has the distinguished position of being the patron saint of cats, even though she may not have even owned one. The reason for this is that her monastery's food was infested with mice. It is said that through prayer, she was able to rid the monastery of mice. If you can get rid of mice, I guess you are a little like a cat in some people's minds, so now she is the patron saint of cats.[75]

St. Gertrude's story calls to mind the classic battle between cat and mouse. In my experience, cats love to play with toys that seem to mimic the movement of mice. Quick, jerking movements allow the cat to crouch down on its hind legs and let thousands of years of feline ferocity pounce onto the unsuspecting toy. If the toy were a real mouse, I doubt it would have much of a chance of surviving.

St. Gertrude did not pounce like a cat on the mice in her monastery, but like a cat catching a mouse, she followed her instincts. She prayed knowing that God has control over his creatures, and he will not suffer his children to starve to death because of some mice. A cat's instinct is to survive; a saint's instinct is to pray.

Another great legend in the history of the church involving cats and the saints is the story of St. Jerome and the Lion. One day, Jerome was teaching at a school when a lion walked into his classroom. Jerome's students had a similar reaction that I would have had and fled the classroom. Jerome noticed, though, that the lion lifted one of its paws in the air and had a thorn stuck into its skin. He removed the thorn and dressed the lion's wound. The lion was healed, and to this day, Saint Jerome is often depicted in Catholic art with a lion.

This story shows a complete one hundred and eighty degree turn in feline behavior when a cat is injured. Veterinarians claim that "Cats tend to hide their illnesses, and they even hide themselves when they're ill. The most common sign of illness in some cats is hiding in a quiet, out-of-the-way place."[76] The lion in St. Jerome's story goes against instinct and seeks out aid. It is not aid from just anyone, though, but of a future saint, a person faithful to God. The lion almost seems to recognize in Jerome a power that can help him, and once again, we see God taking control of the strong of the world and making it subject to the weak.

Finally, there's another story involving a saint and a lion in that of St. Sabas. Sabas was a sixth-century monk in Palestine. One day he went out into the desert to a cave to pray. The cave happened to be the home of a lion. While the saint was praying, the lion entered, and not wanting to disturb the saint's prayers, dragged him gently out of the cave by his clothing. Sabas was not troubled by this and went back into the cave to pray some more. A few moments later, the lion dragged him out of the cave by his clothes again. Finally, Sabas said that this place was big enough for both of them, and after that the lion troubled him no more.

According to the University of Minnesota's College of Biological Sciences, "Lions are highly territorial and occupy the same area for generations."[77] The lion's cave in the story of St. Sabas had probably been its home for years. Instead of running in and defending it to the death, the lion tried peacefully to drag Sabas away, not once, but twice. The lion's ferocity, strength, power, and hunger were once again overcome by a peaceful man devoted to God.

We can see how our spiritual lives are enriched by cats. They demonstrate that they are not just animals with nothing to offer us, but instead help us to increase our faith in God. In all these instances about cats, the people involved had one thing in common, a strong faith. So, cats are the perfect animals for me.

A SORDID HISSTORY

"You know, you can touch a stick of dynamite, but if you touch a venomous snake it'll turn around and bite you and kill you so fast it's not even funny."
—Steve Irwin

hen I was a child, I loved to play with all types of stuffed animals and animal toys. One of my favorites was the rubber snake. I am not sure why I liked a snake toy instead of a cute bunny rabbit or puppy, but looking back on those days, I would probably not be nearly as fearful of snakes as I am today if I had chosen to play with something more cuddly and adorable.

One of the things that people quickly learn when playing with toy snakes is that, even though they are toys, they look real. This can become a problem for those that live in the same house, when you leave them lying on the floor and forget to put them back into the toy box. Many days, I would play with my snake toys and leave them on the floor of the living room or bedroom, or in my parents' room. My family would then leave for some family activity and return after the sun went down. The house would be pitch black and we would have forgotten all about the snakes on the floor. That is, until the light was turned on. Then the screaming started. After a few moments, my dad would stop screaming, calm down, and life would continue on as normal.

Eventually, we became relaxed to the fact that there would be toy snakes on the floor at night. However, because we grew up on a farm in Arkansas, toy snakes were not the only type of snakes that lived in the area, and on occasion, a real snake would get into our home. In these cases, there was not an earplug made in the world that could drown out the blood-curdling scream of my hysterical father.

In order to avoid these situations, my snake toys were banished to my bedroom, hopefully never to be seen by anyone but me. This was okay by me because I was still able to play with them, and even sleep with them at night. At least, that was the case until I awoke one morning to my toy cobra lying on my chest with its life-like cobra head, eyes, and fangs staring into my freshly opened eyes. I still remember that moment vividly: the wood paneling of my bedroom, the red carpet, the screaming and fear that followed. After that experience, my affection for snake toys lessened, and I played with cuter and less frightening animals from then on. I also found that I sound just like my father when I scream in fear.

I believe this is where my uncomfortable feelings toward snakes first originated. However, those feelings of fear and nervousness were also nourished by the stories and legends I learned about snakes from the Bible.

Snakes in the Bible

Snakes truly are frightening creatures to many. Probably one of the reasons for this is that throughout salvation history, they have been a symbol for Satan and evil.[78] The main cause for this comes from the story of Adam and Eve in the Garden. Here is that brief tale from Genesis 3:1–5:

> Now the snake was the most cunning of all the wild animals that the LORD God had made. He asked the woman, "Did God really say, 'You shall not eat from any of the trees in the garden?'" The woman answered the snake: "We may eat of the fruit of the trees in the garden; it is only about the fruit of the tree in the middle of the garden that God said, 'You shall not eat it or even touch it, or else you will die.'" But the snake said to the woman: "You certainly will not die! God knows well that when you eat of it your eyes will be opened and you will be like gods, who know good and evil."

Theologian Pauline A. Vivano helps shed some light on what the serpent represents in this story besides evil. She says,

> In Canaan the serpent was associated with the fertility cults. We know that these cults were a constant source of temptation to Israel, and as indicated in the Old Testament, Israel often succumbed to such temptation. The choice of a serpent to represent the tempter of humanity is the author's way of saying, "Don't get involved with serpents (that is, the fertility cults); they will only cause trouble, as they did for the first man and woman."[79]

In other words, the author of Genesis used the serpent because readers and listeners of the story were familiar with it as a sign of temptation. They would recognize the symbolism of the snake

and know that Adam and Eve were in for a long day. Because of
the snake's association with temptation and evil, it eventually
became identified as the devil, the father of all lies and evil.

Another snaky story is found in Numbers chapter 21. The
Israelites and Moses wander in the desert for forty years on their
way to the Promised Land. Like most folks on a long journey, they
start grumbling about the length of the trip. They complain to
Moses about the food and lack of water on the journey and say
they had it better back in Egypt when they were slaves. Then
the Lord, who has done so much for them, and is continuing
to do so much for them, sends snakes among the people that
bite the Israelites, killing many of them. The Israelites then
decide to stop complaining so much about the journey and
ask Moses to pray to God for their forgiveness. Moses asks for
God's forgiveness, and God tells Moses to build a giant bronze
serpent and mount it on a pole. If anyone is bitten by one of
those snakes, they can now look at the pole and be healed.

A troubling story? Yes! Bible scholar Helen Kenik Mainelli says,
"The healing of the bites is linked to obedience and to faith."[80]
God wants to teach the Israelites to obey and have faith in him,
so by looking at the bronze serpent, they are obeying and trusting
in his healing touch. The bronze snake is also a foreshadowing of
Jesus's death on a cross. All of us who look upon the cross of Jesus
can be healed of our sin and be saved, just as the Israelites were
saved from the poison of the snakes, reminding us that, though
the journey is long, we will end up in the Promised Land.

Snakes found in the New Testament continue the theme of
their being a tad evil. For example, in Luke 11:11 Jesus tells the
disciples how they should pray and how God answers prayers,
when he says, "What father among you would hand his son a
snake when he asks for a fish?"

Scripture Scholar Pablo T. Gadenz comments, "What makes such bold and unrelenting prayer possible is an attitude of filial trust in the Father."[81] Though the snake in this story is seen as an evil and awful gift, it can still be a reminder to us that God knows what we need because he is our Father. If we continue to pray and hope, he will answer our prayers. He will never hand us a snake or something that will harm us, because he is greater than any loving parent.

In Revelation 12:9, a snake is identified as Satan. "The huge dragon, the ancient serpent, who is called the Devil and Satan, who deceived the whole world, was thrown down to earth, and its angels were thrown down with it." Pheme Perkins comments that this passage is linked with Jesus's saying in Luke 10:18: "Jesus said, 'I have observed Satan fall like lightning from the sky.'"[82] These passages confirm that the serpent in the Garden is the same Satan that is in the book of Revelation. They also are the nail in the coffin of snakes being considered evil throughout salvation history.

Most of the remaining Scripture passages that mention snakes portray them as evil or use them to indicate evil in some way or another. For example, multiple times in the Gospel of Matthew, Jesus refers to the Pharisees and Sadducees as vipers. "When he saw many of the Pharisees and Sadducees coming to his baptism, he said to them, 'You brood of vipers! Who warned you to flee from the coming wrath?'" (Matt. 3:7). "You serpents, you brood of vipers, how can you flee from the judgment of Gehenna?" (Matt. 23:33).

But despite all these portrayals of snakes as evil, the Bible also uses the snake to show that God has power over this evil. For example, Mark 16:17–18 says: "These signs will accompany those who believe: in my name they will drive out demons, they will speak new languages. They will pick up serpents [with their hands], and if they drink any deadly thing, it will not harm them. They will lay hands on the sick, and they will recover." The disciples are being commissioned to go out and preach the gospel to the world. Philip Van Linden, CM, says, "The church's missionaries had nothing to fear, because the ascended Lord was with them in their preaching and would confirm their message with special signs of his protection and power."[83]

Some people interpret this verse literally and have started snake-handling churches. They bring poisonous snakes into the congregation and hold them in their hands to show their faith in God. Unfortunately, as many news stories and videos on YouTube illustrate, these snake handlings often end in death. Poisonous snakes are nothing to play around with, and as Brantley Millengan states in an article entitled "Why Don't Catholics Practice Snake Handling?":

> Mark 16.18 does not say that Christians should catch
> poisonous snakes, bring them into churches, and
> hold them as a sign of their faith in God. It simply
> says "they will pick up snakes with their hands." The
> practice of snake-handling adds a great deal to the
> text that is simply not there.[84]

In Acts 28, the Apostle Paul was bitten by a snake but suffered no harm. He was not trying to handle a snake and show it as a sign of faith; he was simply preaching the gospel. Mark 16:18 is once again a commission to us to preach the gospel and not fear what will happen from our preaching. It is not a commission to go pick up poisonous snakes and risk death.

Snakes in the Lives of the Saints

Where should we start, in talking about saints and snakes, if not with the great St. Patrick of Ireland? He must have the most popular snake legend associated with his name. It is said that St. Patrick was once attacked by snakes while praying on a mountain. He then became angry and drove all the snakes off the island of Ireland and into the sea.[85]

This famous story has a special place in my heart, as I once visited the site where Patrick is said to have done it. Croagh Patrick is considered the holiest mountain in Ireland, and is the legendary place where Patrick was fasting when he drove the snakes into the ocean. Pilgrims today can climb a seven-kilometer pilgrim trail up 750 meters that leads to a little chapel that has stood since the fifth century. Once they arrive at the top, they can attend Mass.

I wanted very much to make this pilgrimage. It was late March when we were there, and it was a harsh and rainy day, as many days are on the coast of Ireland. My friend and I started on our journey, only to be defeated by the mountain about halfway up because we were not dressed properly to make it through the wind and cold temperatures. Like the snakes in the story of St. Patrick, we fled down the mountain that day toward the sea. I could not help noticing the resemblance in our story to those poor snakes, and because snakes are a symbol of evil, I took this as God's way of telling me I was banishing some evil from my heart to draw closer to him. The journey was difficult, but I am alive and a better man today for fleeing down the mountain.

Another snake legend takes place in nineteenth-century Italy, in the head of St. John Bosco. In his head? Yes, in his head. St. John had famous dreams and visions that sometimes used animals and creatures to symbolize spiritual virtues and vices, enabling him to understand truths about the state of his spiritual children's souls. In one of these dreams, John and his students were being led by a stranger to a terrifying-looking twenty-foot snake. The stranger told John to dangle a rope over the snake's head and John did. The snake jumped into the rope and became caught in the noose-like loop. The snake tried to free itself but ended up dying in the process. The man then asked John to take the rope and place it in a box. He did as asked and closed the box. The man then told John to watch closely as he reopened the box. Looking in the box, John saw that the rope had turned into the words "Hail Mary." This dream meant that the rope was a symbol for the rosary and the snake for sin and temptation. Through the praying of the Rosary, all sins and temptations can be overcome.[86]

The story of St. John Bosco and the snake rosary calls to mind another story about a snake, the devil, that has played a part in the history of my faith development. I was once speaking with a Benedictine monk who I consider to be a very holy person. He told me a story about the devil, that evil serpent that tricked Adam and Eve in the Garden. Through this story, he was trying to give me advice on avoiding gossip and the temptation to speak ill of people by instead finding something good to say about them. His story went like this:

> There once lived a man who never said an evil word about anyone or anything. People were amazed with his holiness. One man set out to test this holiness. He walked up to the holy man and said, "I have never heard you say an ill word about anyone or anything; I would like to put you to the ultimate test. Can you say anything good about the devil? The holy man thought for a while, then said, "Well, he is a hard worker."

The devil is a hard worker, and like him we have to work hard to avoid the temptation to gossip and speak ill of others. The symbolism of the snake as a rosary and a hard worker can give us a place to flee when we are tempted to commit a sin. So the next time we are driving down the road and see a snake sunning itself on the warm asphalt, instead of jerking the car wheel over and trying to run over it, perhaps we could pray a mystery of the Rosary instead, asking God to help us overcome temptations and grow stronger in our faith.

Another snake story in the lives of the saints involves the fourth-century St. Irene of Thessalonica. Irene preached the faith of Christ faithfully without fear of being persecuted. She was born as the daughter of a pagan king who later converted to Christianity in Persia. It is said that in order to stop her from preaching about Christ, a local prefect of a city had her thrown into a pit of deadly vipers, where she stayed for ten days. While she was in the pit, an angel of the Lord fed her and protected her from harm. After ten days, she was removed from the viper pit completely unharmed. Because of this, more and more people converted to Christ.[87]

This story is in many ways a parallel to Daniel in the lion's den. As with Daniel, an angel protects and watches over St. Irene. The snakes in the story probably very much want to bite her. However, as with the lions in the book of Daniel, the angel keeps the viper's mouths shut. In both cases, at the end of each story, God is praised. In the story of Irene, her impossible escape from the viper pit brings even more people to Christ. Though snakes are considered dangerous and deadly, God still finds a use for them to bring home his lost children. In this light, maybe those snakes aren't as evil as we perceive them to be.

Finally, there is a present-day story about snakes in the Church that involves a recurring miracle. Every year, on the Greek island of Kefalonia between the dates of August 5 and August 15, the Greek Orthodox Church celebrates the Dormition of Mary. During these dates, since 1705, black snakes, European Cat Snakes, appear and make their way to the walls of the church to venerate a silver Icon of Mary called the Panagia Fidousa, or the Virgin of the Snakes. These are normally a very aggressive species of snake, but during the feast of the Dormition of Mary, on this tiny Greek Island, they can be picked up and handled by the faithful and transported to the church so they are not run over by cars on the way.[88]

So, you see, snakes in salvation history have mostly been associated with evil and the devil. But as with all things created by God, if we look hard enough, we can catch a glimpse of the Creator. Things that are considered evil and cause us to tremble in fear, like snakes, can cause us to flee to the only place we know to go when we are in trouble, God's arms. It is a lot easier to catch a glimpse of him from there than from a long way away.

HORSES ARE ROMANTIC?

"Will is to grace as the horse is to the rider."
—St. Augustine of Hippo

I am not very comfortable around horses. They are large, strong animals that carry an intelligence behind their eyes that says, *If you mess with me, I will kick you into next week.*

I grew up on a farm, where our small acreage of beef cattle were moved and corralled by my father holding a five-gallon bucket of cow feed in one hand while yelling, "Who, sook, sook, sook, see calf, come on," with the other pressed against the side of his mouth in the shape of a crude half megaphone. I have no clue as to the origins of this cattle call, but its effectiveness not only conditioned the cows to come to the pen and eat, but it also negated the use of horses to aid us on our farm. Because of this, my lack of experience around horses allows me to be perfectly content to let the noble steed have its space and an entire pasture to roam around in if that is what it would like.

Not only am I uncomfortable around horses, but I also do not understand the mystique of the horse. Horses are beautiful creatures and should be admired for their importance to humans throughout history. Nevertheless, my lack of experience around them, followed by these other stories I am about to share, leave me confused as to why women seem to love horses so much and why horses are considered so romantic.

When I was a younger man, I remember going on a date to a film entitled *The Nights of Rodanthe*. This film was adapted from a book by author Nicholas Sparks. His books usually have a romantic and sad quality to them, so I knew the girl I was going on a date with would enjoy it, while I would be in complete misery. There were about twenty-five people in the theater: twenty-three women, me, and an older man who came with his wife. As the film progressed, I found myself paying attention to the sounds of the people seated around me more than the actual film. Gasps, sniffles, and snorts formed an ambient soundtrack to the show that built up as the movie progressed into a final dam-bursting crescendo of tears.

I have no problem with people having these emotions during a film. However, what really had me scratching my head the most about this show was the ending. Here is a semi-spoiler alert unless you have not seen this movie in the past ten years. At the end, the camera pans to a lonely, empty beach. Suddenly, a stampede of wild horses appears seemingly out of nowhere and gallops across the sands in a strange sort of majestic mess. If the moviegoers were not already crying at that point, the random herd of wild horses opened the floodgates.

Years later, I remember being on a beach vacation and seeing advertisements for moonlight horse rides on the beach.. I just did not get it. The only time I have ever ridden a horse I was absolutely miserable. The saddle was uncomfortable, and the horse had his own agenda about where he wanted to go, followed by a flatulence problem that plagued us the entire ride, making the experience extremely unpleasant. I cannot imagine riding a horse under those same circumstances, even or especially on a dark beach in the middle of the night.

So why do people seem to be so in love with the horse? Lucy Cavendish, in an article titled "Why We Love Horses," helped enlighten me. She says:

> Women have love affairs with horses. We kiss their warm soft noses and trim their quivering whiskers. We brush them and plait them and paint their hooves with shiny oil. We bathe them and rub them and rug them and buy matching accessories for them. We give them garlic to eat to ward off colds and molasses in their feed to keep them healthy. We heat bran mashes to warm them up in winter. We make their manes and tails look neat and put boots on them so they don't hurt their legs. We talk about them as if they are husbands or lovers or babies. We call them 'my boy' and 'my lad' and 'he' as in, 'he doesn't like it when...' and, 'ooh, my boy's in a bad mood today.' I know women who spend every penny they earn on their horses. They spend their weekends and evenings cleaning tack, and mucking out, and stringing up hay nets, and grooming, and then, finally, riding; because it's not just about the riding, it's about being with them, looking after them, being near them."[89]

Horse lover Molly Watson also has this to say:

> What is it with women and horses? Why do so many of us love them so much? I think it may have something to do with both power and powerlessness. To ride a horse and have it do as you ask, despite the difference in brute strength, is to feel powerful. But no matter how brave the rider, that power can only be accessed by

persuasion — and perhaps this is a particularly female gift. The experiences I had with horses in my teens delayed my interest in boys and provided me with a useful precursor for later romantic entanglements. Horses are the ultimate strong and silent types, they let themselves be fussed over without any evidence they love you back.[90]

These are beautiful descriptions. I now understand a little more about why some people honor and romanticize the horse so much. The horse is, for many, a reminder of how to love and be loved.

Horses in the Bible

Throughout Scripture, love is not the symbol chosen to symbolize the horse. Instead, the horse is mentioned in relation to war and is usually a symbol for strength.[91] A prime example of this is found in the book of Job's description of a war-horse. Job 39:19 says, "Do you give the horse his strength, and clothe his neck with a mane?" Elsewhere in the Old Testament, when horses are mentioned in great numbers, it is usually to symbolize the strength of a person or an invading army. These people or armies end up relying on strength that comes from the world and not on God's strength. Because of this, the worldly end up losing what power they had to begin with.

For example, in 1 Kings 5:6, King Solomon, one of the wisest men in all the Bible, is described as having a great multitude of horses. "Solomon had forty thousand stalls for horses for chariots and twelve thousand horsemen." This multitude may seem like a great thing for Israel, but in the book of Deuteronomy Moses explains what rules Israel needs to follow once they get settled into the Promised Land to stay faithful to God and his commandments. One of the rules he states for the future king is found in Deuteronomy 17:16: "But he shall not have a great number of horses; nor shall he make his people go back again to Egypt to acquire many horses, for the LORD said to you, Do not go back that way again."

Scripture scholar Leslie J. Hoppe, OFM, comments that "what makes Israel's monarchy unique is the subjection of the king to the law. Like every other Israelite, the king, too, is to order his life according to the book of the Law. This is an important check on the monarchy's inherent tendency toward absolutism. Obedience to the law will lead to the maintenance of the king, while disobedience will surely lead to disaster."[92] The fact that Solomon had so many horses was a sign that he was not following God's commands. Not following God eventually led to Solomon's downfall and the division of the kingdom of Israel. "So the LORD said to Solomon: Since this is what you want, and you have not kept my covenant and the statutes which I enjoined on you, I will surely tear the kingdom away from you and give it to your servant" (1 Kings 11:11). If Solomon had remembered the words of David, his father, about horses in Psalm 20:8, it could have been a reminder to him of how a king of Israel is truly to rule. "Some rely on chariots, others on horses, but we on the name of the LORD our God."

In chapter fourteen of the book of Exodus, the Bible again shows us that though a multitude of horses may symbolize strength, that strength is no match for the power of God. Moses and the Israelites are on the run from Pharaoh and the Egyptian army. Moses stretches out his arms and God parts the Red Sea, and the Israelites are able to pass through the sea on dry land. Pharaoh and his army of horses and chariots follow the Israelites into the sea. Exodus 14:23 specifically states, "The Egyptians followed in pursuit after them—all Pharaoh's horses and chariots and horsemen—into the midst of the sea." Once the Israelites are safe, Moses, by God's command, again stretches out his arm and the sea closes, swallowing Pharaoh's army in the waters.

Scripture scholar John F. Craghan comments that "the returning waters then engulf the entire Egyptian army."[93] By stating in Exodus 14:23 that all of Pharaoh's horses, chariots, and horsemen went into the sea, the author of Exodus shows us that Pharaoh relied on earthly might to conquer the Israelites. The Israelites' strength, however, did not come from any number of horses or chariots; instead, it came from God. God shows through the parting of the Red Sea and the drowning of Pharaoh's powerful army that God has power over his creation. We, like the Israelites, should place our trust in him, not in the strength of horses as did Pharaoh.

Horses continue to symbolize strength and war as well as a few other things in Scripture during the end of the world, known as the Apocalypse. In Revelation 6:1–8, the four horsemen of the apocalypse are released to bring plagues upon the earth.

> Then I watched while the Lamb broke open the first of the seven seals, and I heard one of the four living creatures cry out in a voice like thunder, "Come forward." I looked, and there was a white horse, and its rider had a bow. He was given a crown, and he rode forth victorious to further his victories.
>
> When he broke open the second seal, I heard the second living creature cry out, "Come forward." Another horse came out, a red one. Its rider was given power to take peace away from the earth, so

that people would slaughter one another. And he was given a huge sword.

When he broke open the third seal, I heard the third living creature cry out, "Come forward."I looked, and there was a black horse, and its rider held a scale in his hand. I heard what seemed to be a voice in the midst of the four living creatures. It said, "A ration of wheat costs a day's pay, and three rations of barley cost a day's pay. But do not damage the olive oil or the wine."

When he broke open the fourth seal, I heard the voice of the fourth living creature cry out, "Come forward." I looked, and there was a pale green horse. Its rider was named Death, and Hades accompanied him. They were given authority over a quarter of the earth, to kill with sword, famine, and plague, and by means of the beasts of the earth.

There is a white horse, a red horse, a black horse, and a pale green horse. The figure on the white horse is said to symbolize Christ, while the figures on the red, black, and pale green horses are said to symbolize war, famine, and death.[94] Once again, we can see that the horse is a symbol of strength because Christ, the white horse, is the ultimate source of strength, while famine and death are a result of war.

These horses and horsemen are similar to those referenced by the Prophet Zechariah in Zechariah 6:1–8: "Again I raised my eyes and saw four chariots coming out from between two mountains; and the mountains were of bronze. The first chariot had red horses, the second chariot black horses, the third chariot white horses, and the fourth chariot dappled horses—all of them strong. . . ." Again, they seem to be patrolling in a warlike fashion, to use their strength to try and bring peace to the land. Strength and war are once again front and center in the mentioning of the horses and horsemen.

Horses in the Lives of Saints

The seventh-century patron saint of horses is St. Eligius of Noyon. It is said that Eligius was having difficulty shoeing a horse one day, and in order to put the shoe on more easily, he miraculously removed the leg of the horse from its body, put the horseshoe on, then placed the leg back on the horse's body. Don't try this at home, or on the farm, folks. On December 1, the Church celebrates Saint Eligius's feast day, and in some places in the world, horses can still receive a blessing to celebrate this day.

In my state of Arkansas, a local priest still blesses horses at a local horse racing track named Oaklawn. Fr. James West, a local priest, goes out to the stables and sprinkles the horses with Holy Water while reciting the traditional St. Francis of Assisi blessing of animals prayer.[95] This prayer is not specific to any one animal species. The most common and specific blessing for horses and draft animals actually asks for the intercession of fourth-century St. Anthony the Abbot. Here is that blessing:

> The animals praise and glorify God inasmuch as they assist man and serve him. In their own way they assist man in attaining his ultimate goal, and for that reason the Church blesses them. In her blessing the church commends these animals to St. Anthony the hermit, who from the earliest times was regarded as the patron of farmers and animal breeders. The following prayers can be used when the animals are placed in harness for the first time. O God, our

refuge and strength, the source of our devotion, hear the devout prayers of the Church, grant that what we ask in faith we may obtain in fact.

Almighty, eternal God, who didst test glorious Saint Anthony the hermit in many temptations and didst grant him to go forth untouched by the seductions of this world: grant us Thy servants to make progress in virtue by his example and to be freed from the dangers of this life by his merits and intercession.

May these animals, O Lord, receive Thy blessing; may they be sound in body and, by the intercession of Saint Anthony the hermit, may they be preserved from all evil. Through Christ our Lord. Amen.[96]

Because the main job of the horse is to carry a rider, it makes sense for the Church to also have a patron saint of horsemen or horseback riders. That is St. Martin of Tours. This fourth-century saint was a Roman soldier who was riding a horse one day when he came across a beggar freezing to death on the side of the road. Having only the clothes on his back to give, Martin cut half of his beautiful officer's cloak from his uniform and gave it to the beggar. Later that night, Jesus, surrounded by angels, visited Martin in a dream and said to the angels, "Martin, who is not even baptized yet, has wrapped Me in his own cloak."[97]

Soldiers like Martin hunted, battled, traveled, and raced on horseback. The horse was an extension of the soldier, bringing terror, speed, war, or in the case of Martin, peace and love to the people he met. In the story of St. Martin, one can hear an echo of the great prophet Isaiah proclaiming, "How beautiful upon the mountains are the feet of the one bringing good news, Announcing peace, bearing good news, announcing salvation, saying to Zion, 'Your God is King!' " (Isa. 52:7). Only, instead of feet, hooves were bringing the good news Martin had to share. How many other saints in the history of the Church have been carried to and from distant locations by a horse to spread the good news and love of the gospel?

Another great horse tradition is the breeding of a horse called the Cartujano, a type of Andalusian. These horses began being bred in the 1400s by Carthusian monks. They are a very rare breed; only about 500 purebred Cartujano horses are still in existence today because the breed was nearly devastated by the French invasion of Spain and the resulting war for independence in 1810.[98]

Horse experts describe this breed as the Horse of Kings. It is said to have a personality that is "noble, docile and well-balanced."[99] It seems to follow that an intelligent animal such as this should take on the characteristics of its breeders. Carthusian monks focus on the essential characteristics in their daily lives of solitude and a mixture of community life. This mix of solitude and community produces a life of simplicity and peacefulness, as well as kinship with one another. Their way of life is neither too introverted nor extroverted, but it is a balanced mix, like the personality of the Cartujano horse. If anyone ever says that the way you treat an animal does not matter, point them to the Cartujano horse.

Throughout the history of Scripture and the lives of the Catholic saints, horses have been a sign of strength and a sign of sacrifice by giving us their strength to carry us on our journey. Sometimes, they have even shown us that horsepower is not the only type of strength one needs, but rather, the strength of faith in God. I hope that they continue to assist our pilgrimage on earth by helping us spread the gospel in their own way. I also hope that they continue to tug at the heartstrings of many couples, helping them to find love and adventure in the strangest of places.

MY BEST FRIEND

*"All his life he tried to be a good person.
Many times, however, he failed. For after all, he was
only human. He wasn't a dog."*
—CHARLES M. SCHULZ

Several of my best friends are Catholic priests. Whenever I go out to eat with them, I always try to sit on their right side so that I can say, "It looks like I am seated at the right hand of the father." I have said this so many times that I no longer get laughs, but eye rolls. The reason I say it is because every Sunday at Mass during the Nicene Creed, we Catholics proclaim that Jesus is seated at the right hand of God the Father in heaven. In the Bible, to be seated at someone's right hand is a big deal: it is a place of honor, closeness, and power.

In the animal kingdom, I firmly believe that dogs sit at our right hand. They are faithful, loving, trusting, obedient, and childlike. Dogs know and obey their masters' call and are not prone to anger unless something unjust is being done to them. In a very strange way, they are a model of faith for how to live a Christian life. Like the dog, we need a faithful, loving, trusting, obedient, childlike relationship with God so we can hear our Father's call and live the life he truly wants us to live.

Dogs are also wonderful companions on our pilgrimage here on earth. Recently, my wife and I were on a flight to Dallas, Texas. The woman sitting behind us had two dogs traveling under my wife's seat. They did not move or make a sound for the entire flight, and we had no clue they were there until we began exiting the plane and saw the dogs sitting in their owner's lap. The woman said, "I take them everywhere. Their tickets cost more than mine!"

I once owned a beautiful Golden Retriever named Brinkley. Every place I went, he would want to go and experience what I was doing. If I went fishing, he would go, and because he was a retriever, he would chase my fishing lure and hook out into the water and get tangled up in the line. Thankfully, I never caught him with the hook. My heart was broken when I would drive off without him to some place that he could not go, leaving him standing in the driveway staring at me with those sad, brown, puppy-dog eyes. I loved him so much. He was my best friend.

Like me and the woman on the plane, some people have to take their dogs everywhere they go because they are their best friends. This sometimes leads to amazing stories of dogs becoming lost and finding their way hundreds of miles back to their owners' homes. Other times, you can see people chasing dogs and screaming their names down the street with a leash trailing in their puppy's wake, trying desperately to catch up so it does not become lost.

Sadly, my dog Brinkley was eventually stolen out of my parents' yard, never to be seen again. My heart was crushed and so were the hearts of the rest of my family. I lost him and would go to almost any length to find him. I searched for days and weeks for my little buddy, but no matter where I looked, I never found him. Though he has never returned, these thoughts of Brinkley and people trying to find their lost dogs remind me of Jesus coming after that one lost sheep and the prodigal son returning home to his father after being away for a very long time. When I think of what I would go through to save or find my furry little friend, there is hope in my heart that God loves me infinitely more the same exact way.

Dogs in the Bible

When beginning a study of dogs in Scripture, one discovers quickly that dogs do not have much of a presence there. They are mentioned more in passing by Bible characters, and in some cases, they even have their actions mimicked by those characters. Unfortunately for dog lovers, this next sentence is going to come across as a gut punch: Dogs in the Bible are represented as filthy, unclean, and loathsome.[100]

In the book of Judges chapter 7, God helps Gideon defeat the Midianite army in a battle. The Midianites were a group of nomads who took over and oppressed Israel and reduced God's people to absolute poverty. The people of Israel cry out to God to help and free them from the Midianites. God hears their prayers and uses Gideon as his instrument of deliverance. However, God does not want Israel to attribute the defeat of Midian to themselves or to Gideon, but to him alone. Therefore, God tells Gideon to lessen the number of soldiers in his army so they will know it was God who delivered Midian into Israel's hands.

How did Gideon do this? First, before the battle, he told his soldiers that if anyone was afraid, they could leave. Twenty-two thousand of the thirty-two thousand soldiers left Gideon, and only ten thousand fighting men remained. God then told Gideon that there were still too many soldiers and that more needed to be dismissed. To thin their numbers this time, God told Gideon to take his men to a stream for a drink of water. The ones who lapped up water with their tongues like dogs should stay and fight, while the ones who cupped water in their hands to drink should be dismissed back to their homes. There were three hundred men who drank water like a dog and nine thousand seven hundred who drank with their hands cupped. Gideon took these three hundred men who drank like dogs and defeated the entire Midianite army.

It is hard to understand why God had the soldiers drink like dogs to prove who would and would not be chosen to battle for Israel. Scripture scholar John A. Grindel, CM, posits that "It may have been an arbitrary test to provide a means by which God can make a selection." George Haydock mentions that this test could be related to an old proverb that says, "'The dog drinks and flees away,' alluding to the dogs of Egypt, who, through fear of the crocodiles which infest the banks of the Nile, lap the water with all expedition, 'like a dog from the Nile.'"[101] This would imply that drinking like a dog is a sign of cowardice, and therefore God chose the three hundred weakest soldiers in Gideon's army to fight in the battle, showing that God can use the weakest among us to do amazing things.

In the New Testament, in Luke 16:19–21, dogs are the only creatures that will have anything to do with the poor man Lazarus. "There was a rich man who dressed in purple garments and fine linen and dined sumptuously each day. And lying at his door was a poor man named Lazarus, covered with sores, who would gladly have eaten his fill of the scraps that fell from the rich man's table. Dogs even used to come and lick his sores."

Biblical scholar Pablo T. Gadnez states that because Lazarus was "covered with sores, he was probably accursed. Adding insult to injury were the dogs."[102] This was considered an insult because dogs in ancient times were considered unclean. Leviticus 11:27 says, "Also by the various quadrupeds that walk on paws; they are unclean for you." Dogs in the Bible are not the cute, well-trained house dogs that we raise and love today. Instead, they roamed in packs, part feral, scavenging and spreading diseases. The dogs coming to lick at Lazarus's sores were just the icing on the cake of his other problems. The presence of the licking dogs confirms he is in the lowest of possible circumstances in this parable.

Not to be forgotten in Scripture is the dogs' ancestor the wolf. The wolf in Scripture is characterized by "treachery, ferocity, and bloodthirstiness."[103] In the Gospel of Matthew 7:15, Jesus tells his disciples, "Beware of false prophets, who come to you in sheep's clothing, but underneath are ravenous wolves." Similarly, in Acts 20:29, St. Paul declares, "I know that after my departure savage wolves will come among you, and they will not spare the flock."

Daniel J. Harrington, SJ, comments that the wolves are the people who lead Israel astray in the Gospel of Matthew and later are used to describe situations in the early church in Acts.[104] In both instances, it is easy to see that the wolf is not an image of great majesty and beauty like the ones we see in beautiful pictures today, but a savage, wild, hungry beast, ready to devour those who try to stay faithful to God.

Dogs in the Lives of Saints

Here, finally, we break with the biblical tradition of dogs as loathsome and unclean. When encountering the holy men and women of the past two millennia, dogs show us that they can indeed be faithful, loving, relatively clean!, and kind.

One type of dog, the Saint Bernard, played such a role in the life of eleventh-century Saint Bernard of Montjoux that the species derives its name from him. It is said that St. Bernard traveled around mountain towns in the Swiss Alps administering the Sacraments to the faithful. In every town he entered, he heard stories of people freezing to death or being attacked by robbers, so he took it upon himself to do something about it. He set up two hospices, run by Augustinian monks, for shelter and safety for weary travelers in the mountains. From these hospices, every day, the monks would set out with huge dogs to track and find missing people in the mountains.[105] These dogs eventually were bred to be the Saint Bernard that we know and love, with a personality that could almost be said to be saintly. They are gentle, calm, and patient dogs that are faithful to their owners and love children. Because of their enormous size, they are also able to watch over and protect from outside dangers. Those characteristics sound very much like those of a saint, with a personality of patience, gentleness, and kindness toward others, as well as the ability to step in and intercede for us when we may need it.

St. Roch was a fourteenth-century Franciscan saint who is also the patron saint of dogs. The following story is the reason he is our canine friends' patron today. In 1315, in Acquapendente, a town in northern Italy, an epidemic broke out. Many in the town were afflicted with the disease and sent to the town hospital where St. Roch worked night and day to ease the people's suffering and, at times, miraculously curing the disease with the Sign of the Cross. After the disease was under control in Acquapendente, Roch then traveled to Rome to help out with another epidemic that had begun there. He cured and helped many in Rome and other towns, until he finally arrived at Piacenza. There he was stricken with the very disease he had been fighting against so passionately. In order not to be a burden to the townsfolk, he went and lived in the woods. A dog is said to have carried him bread daily from a neighboring home for his survival, and slowly he regained his strength and was healed. Because of this faithful dog, St. Roch is now forever associated with our canine friends.[106]

This beautiful story of St. Roch receiving the literal bread of life from a dog reminds me of my beloved Aunt Betty. She is a Eucharistic Minister in the Catholic Church and takes Holy

Communion to those who are unable to attend Mass because of illness or other situations. Similar to the story of the dog in the life of St. Roch, my aunt takes the bread of life to hungry souls so that they too may live and draw closer to God.

A dog also played a huge role in turning the life of Margaret of Cortona into that of a saint. This thirteenth-century Italian woman lived for nine years out of wedlock with a man and bore him a son. She longed for a life of purity but was unable to commit to it. One day, she was waiting for her boyfriend, Arsenio, and was met by his dog instead. The dog is said to have led her into the forest where she found that Arsenio had been killed.[107] This began for her a life of penance and sanctity. If the dog had not led her into the woods to find Arsenio's body, she may have never learned the truth of his fate and changed her life.

The story of St. Margaret of Cortona can seem similar to what we call today "cadaver dogs." These dogs are actually trained to smell death and detect human remains. These dogs have a rather sad job, but in a way, they can still bring peace to families searching for lost loved ones. They help families and people find closure and continue on with their lives to greater things, similar to St. Margaret.

One of the most remarkable stories in the history of the Church that involves a dog, is the story of St. John Bosco and his dog, Grigio. John Bosco is the founder of the Salesian Order, an order that is basically devoted to Catholic Youth Ministry. One evening, John was walking home and was attacked by two men. Out of nowhere, a huge gray dog appeared and jumped onto John's attackers. The men begged John to call the dog off. He made them promise not to commit these crimes again and prayed for them before the men were finally permitted to run away. It is said that from that time on, Grigio showed up whenever John was in trouble. Eyewitnesses saw Grigio protecting St. John for nearly thirty more years! John was asked about the dog and he said, "It sounds ridiculous to call him an angel, yet he is no ordinary dog."[108]

Dog expert Marieta Murg has this to say about why dogs are so protective of their owners: "By developing such strong bonds with your dog, as time goes by, you become a part of his family just as much as he becomes a part of yours. His instinctive need to protect is established and reinforced through mutual trust and guidance. If someone threatens you or your family, the dog will react and become defensive."[109] In the circumstance of Grigio and John Bosco, the dog would appear when St. John was in danger or in an insecure situation, showing him as a type of guardian over him. Because of this, maybe it doesn't sound so ridiculous to call Grigio or our dogs guardian angels for us.

Finally, on a trip to Rome and the Vatican, I came across one of the greatest stories of dogs, or in this case a wolf, in Christian history. I was walking along by my hotel when I noticed a tile on the curb of a sidewalk. The tile depicted a Franciscan friar and a huge wolf. I knew enough of Catholic history to know the Franciscan was probably St. Francis of Assisi, but I was not sure why the wolf was on the tile. So, I did a little investigating and found out the story.

In the town of Gubbio, Italy, there lived a wolf that was attacking and killing livestock and people. The townspeople tried many things, but they could not stop the animal from killing. So they sought the aid of St. Francis. Francis listened to them and agreed to help as best as he could. Fearlessly, he went out into the woods to meet the wolf. When the wolf came into view it immediately began to stalk Francis like one of its prey. Francis looked at the wolf and said, "Come Brother Wolf, I will not hurt you. Let us talk in peace." The wolf then sat down and listened intently to Francis.

Francis asked the wolf to tell him why he was attacking the people and the livestock. The wolf explained that he was hungry and wanted to eat. Francis then began to pray for hours and finally, when he stopped, he looked at the wolf and said that he had a solution. He said that in exchange for not killing the livestock of the townspeople, the wolf could be fed by the townspeople, on the condition that the wolf repented of what he had done. The wolf placed his paw on Francis's hand and agreed. Francis and the wolf walked back to Gubbio together, and when they arrived at the town Francis told the townspeople all that had transpired between him and the wolf. He also told them that the wolf asked for their forgiveness. The townsfolk agreed with Francis and the wolf on the terms of the arrangement and from then on, the people of Gubbio took care of the wolf, and he acted as their defender against outside foes. The townspeople cared for Brother Wolf for two years before he passed away.[110]

As I reflect on the story of Francis and the wolf, so many things catch my attention. In the midst of all the amazing events happening, St. Francis is really trying to understand why the wolf is doing what it is doing and help it correct his behavior. Francis and the wolf can teach us that when we try to understand why someone is acting the way they are, we have a chance of saving them instead of writing them off as a lost cause.

Dogs are some of the best friends some of us will ever have. They truly sit at our right hand to guard us, guide us, and love us. Though their reputation in the Bible is not pristine, they continue to bring joy in our lives and the lives of countless saints throughout the ages by not being simply companions on our journey, but by being our best friends.

BIRDS OF PRAY

"Empty yourself completely; sit waiting, content with God's gift, like a little chick tasting and eating nothing but what its mother brings."
—Brief Rule of Saint Romuald

In my family, we have an aunt whom we jokingly, but lovingly, call Saint Betty the Little Crepe Myrtle of Charleston. This is a play on the name of St. Thérèse the Little Flower of Lisieux, but our humor is not far from the truth. Aunt Betty is, in my opinion, a living saint.

Ever since I was a child growing up in Charleston, Arkansas, I can remember Aunt Betty giving to her family and the local community unselfishly and without reserve, never expecting anything in return. No matter where we were going, or what we were doing, if we were riding with her in her "Apple Brown Betty" colored Chevy Astro van, she was encouraging her daughters, nieces, and nephews to pray the Rosary along with a group of cloistered nuns on a worn-out cassette tape. If one of us had a particularly bad day, she would tell us that things would be okay because, "God has a plan for you." Her example to me growing up helped shape my faith today.

Today, as I age, and my faith in God hopefully matures, I am curious how God works in the lives of people that I consider holy. One day, I was blessed enough to learn how my Aunt Betty sees God working in her life, and her faith life involves birds.

Aunt Betty told me that many years ago when my grandmother passed away, my grandfather did not want to live in his home all by himself. He needed to be around people that he loved, so he moved out to my Aunt Betty's house in the country. As they settled in, they found that one of their favorite activities together was watching the St. Louis Cardinals' baseball games on television.

After my grandfather grew ill and passed away, one day Aunt Betty was looking out the window and witnessed several beautiful cardinals sitting on a tree directly outside the window looking back at her. She said this was a sign to her that her dad was watching from heaven and that he was still with her in this life. Now, every time she looks outside and notices a blur of red feathers hurtle past her window, or spots a group of cardinals sunning themselves on a barbed wire fence on a hot summer day, her faith in God is renewed, and the joy of the reunion she will have with my grandfather in heaven is also remembered.

Birds in the Bible

This is just a small example of how God uses his creation to speak to us in ways that we cannot begin to comprehend. Our feathered friends, the birds, are one of these voices, and they have a history in Scripture of pointing our eyes to the holy.[111]

One example of this is the story of Noah's ark found in chapters 6–8 of the book of Genesis. Noah found a pragmatic use for birds as he drifted around the flooded world on the ark for many months.

With no way of knowing when the world would be hospitable for him, his family, or the animals riding in the ark after the flood waters began to recede, Noah would periodically pop the top hatch of the ark and let a dove or raven fly into the sky. If it returned to him, that meant there was nowhere for the bird to land, and consequently, it was a sign that the appointed time had not come for Noah or anyone else on the ark to disembark.

Finally, one day, a dove was released, and it returned to Noah with an olive leaf in its mouth. This meant the waters had receded greatly and Noah could almost return to dry land. Noah then waited seven more days and released another dove. This time the bird did not return to him at all. Because of this, Noah knew the flood waters had receded enough for the bird to leave the ark and find a new home. But he, his family, and the other animals waited on the ark until God told them that they could leave the ark (Gen. 8:16). As theologian Pauline A. Viviano states, "It is God who tells Noah to leave the ark; Noah does not rely on information gained from sending out of the bird."[112])

In this example, the birds help guide Noah's eyes to God. After spending months in a smelly, cramped boat on turbulent seas, he had to have been ready to hurl himself overboard and swim to the nearest land possible. However, the reason God had flooded the earth was that "the earth was corrupt in the view of God and full of lawlessness" (Gen. 6:11). The disappearance of the bird reminded Noah to wait on God's commands and be patient, because not obeying God leads to corruption and sin.

In Exodus 19:4, a specific bird, the eagle, not only points our gaze to the Holy, but it also becomes an actual symbolic representation of God.[113] "You have seen how I treated the Egyptians and how I bore you up on eagles' wings and brought you to myself." God uses the imagery of an eagle's wings to describe how he broke the chains of the Israelites' slavery from Egypt and then carried them away to the long-awaited Promised Land.

If you have witnessed an eagle in flight, an appropriate way to describe it would be slow and steady. Eagle experts Jon M. Gerrard and Gary R. Bortolotti write, "Eagles are capable of sustained flapping flight but they usually spend little time doing it." In fact, one female eagle they studied averaged two minutes of flapping flight per one hour. The reason for this approach to their flight is that "It takes a lot of energy to flap such large wings."[114]

The Israelites who were wandering for forty years in the wilderness to reach the Promised Land probably felt as if God was beating his wings for two minutes every year to reach their appointed destination. However, they had to wait on God and be patient. When God says, "I bore you up on eagles' wings and brought you to myself," a person with the understanding of how eagles fly can see an allusion to the way the Israelites were brought out of the land of Egypt, a slow and steady flight that led to the Promised Land.

In Proverbs 27:8 a bird is not used to symbolize God, but instead, to impart what can happen if we abandon God. "Like a bird far from the nest, so is anyone far from home." The intent of Proverbs is to impart wisdom. At first glance, this verse seems to be a great movie quote or a popular slogan to hang on a wall. Once again, though, the bird directs our gaze past the worldly to something infinitely deeper.

The nest is the bird's home. It is the place where it is raised, fed, kept warm, and even learns to fly. Life for the bird is safe at home, snuggled inside the nest away from the world. It is when the bird decides to leave the nest that countless dangers can strike, and the further away it is from home, the longer it takes to return to the safety of home.

This one small sentence from Proverbs brought to my mind an important moment I had as a teenager that involved a bird. I was traveling home one night from my Aunt Betty's home on a bumpy country highway when I heard a loud thud on my car door. I immediately slammed on my brakes. I sat there for a few moments trying to slow my heartbeat and catch my breath. When I opened the car door and stepped out into the clear night air, I found what had crashed into my car: a beautiful owl. This sad occasion was the first time I had ever laid eyes on an owl in the wild. My heart felt as if it had broken into a thousand pieces. This was one of the most beautiful animals I had ever had the pleasure of seeing. With red, teary eyes, I carried the owl off of the road.

I was upset about this incident for a long time, and it taught me how dangerous it can be for an animal to stray away from the nest. However, it was not until I contemplated the sentence from the book of Proverbs, along with my experience with that beautiful owl, that I realized how much my nest is God, and when I stray from him, like the owl, I am placing my life in mortal danger. My sad incident with this bird acts as a map for me today, reminding me to alter my flight path and head back to the nest when I have flown too far from God.

In the New Testament, birds continue to point our eyes heavenward to God, but in some instances, they do this by showing us how God comes down to us. Matthew 3:13–17 relates the Baptism of Jesus in the Jordan River. In this scene, John the Baptist beholds the "Spirit of God descending like a dove [and] coming upon him." Once again, as in Exodus 19:4, a bird is used to describe how God interacts with us; however, instead of a powerful and majestic eagle, a small, quiet, beautiful white dove is used symbolically to describe God in this link to his people.

Fr. Daniel Harrington writes, "The description of the Spirit's descent is presented in an adverbial phrase, ('dove like = like a dove does) that may evoke the Old Testament creation account ('the Spirit of God was moving over the face of the waters,' Gen. 1:2)."[115] In other words, the phrase "like a dove" demonstrates one way in which the Spirit comes to us not only in the New Testament, but also throughout all of salvation history. This is why the Holy Spirit is so often portrayed as a dove in Christian art.[116]

In Luke 12:6–7, Jesus uses a sparrow to convey to us how much we are loved by God and to trust that if he can care about a tiny, seemingly insignificant bird, infinitely more does he love us: "Are not five sparrows sold for two small coins? Yet not one of them has escaped the notice of God. Even the hairs of your head have all been counted. Do not be afraid. You are worth more than many sparrows."

The common house sparrow weighs about 0.9–1.1 ounces.[117] In two of the passages of Scripture that we previously studied, Exodus 19:4 and Matthew 3:16, God uses an eagle and a dove to symbolically describe himself. It would take over one hundred sparrows to add up to the average weight of a Bald Eagle (105.8–222.2 oz.), and about four sparrows to add up to the weight of a small Mourning Dove (3.4–6.0 oz.).[118] A sparrow is very tiny. The birds describing God are so much greater than the one used to describe us. Does that mean that God is so great and big that he does not care for us? Thankfully, Jesus tells us that we may feel tiny and insignificant like the sparrow, but we are loved by a God infinitely more than we can imagine. No person—unborn, young, adult, or elderly—is forgotten by God. How honored the bird is to represent not only God, but also his unending and undying love for us.

Birds in the Lives of Saints

Birds are also present in the lives of Catholic saints, and as in Scripture, they too have a way of pointing our eyes to heaven. For example, in the year AD 236, Pope St. Anterus had just passed away, and the Roman clergy assembled to elect a new pope. While the priests gathered, a dove flew among the crowd of people and landed atop the head of an unknown layperson named Fabian. The conclave saw this as a sign of the Holy Spirit's favor and elected Fabian the new Pope. Those gathered to elect the new pope at the conclave did not select Fabian because of the dove alone. The men who were gathered recalled Matthew 3:16, and how the Holy Spirit descended upon Jesus like a dove after his baptism.[119] The dove was a clear sign to the conclave that the Holy Spirit had chosen Fabian to be the next Vicar of Christ on Earth.

The Voyage of Saint Brendan tells the story of Brendan the Navigator and his group of sixth-century Irish monks as they set out on a seven-year voyage around the world to find the Garden of Eden. This fifteen-hundred-year-old story has everything from enormous sheep, fireball-throwing giants, and talking birds.[120] The birds in the story not only point St. Brendan's eyes and heart to God, but they also do it in a way that thousands of Christian men and women throughout history have also done, by praying the Divine Office or the Liturgy of the Hours.

If you are unfamiliar with the Liturgy of the Hours, the United States Conference of Catholic Bishops defines it as "the Work of God (*Opus Dei*) . . . the daily prayer of the Church, marking the hours of each day and sanctifying the day with prayer."[121] At different times during the day: morning (6 a.m.), mid-morning (9 a.m.), midday (noon), afternoon (3 p.m.), evening (6 p.m.), and night (9 p.m.), Christians get together and pray psalms and Scripture passages to saturate their day with Scripture.

In *The Voyage of Saint Brendan*, Brendan visits an island called the Paradise of Birds where he happens upon a tree full of talking white birds. These birds, along with Brendan and his fellow monks, worship the Lord together in one language by singing, chanting, and praising God throughout the day in their own man and bird version of the Liturgy of the Hours. At 6 a.m. they chant, "May the radiance of the Lord, our God be upon us!" Nine a.m. brings forth beak and mouth to sing, "Sing praises to our God, sing praises! Sing praises to our king. Sing praises in wisdom." For the midday hour they pray, "Shine your countenance, Lord, upon us, and have mercy on us." At 3 p.m., Nones, they chant, "How good and pleasant it is that brothers live together as one." And 6 p.m. prayer brings the song, "A hymn is due to thee, O God, in Zion, and a vow shall be paid to you in Jerusalem." Life on the island goes on like this for several days.[122]

The next time we hear a bird singing outside our window, we could call to mind the angelic praises that Brendan and the birds sang to God on that island, and with them, add a little song of our own to praise our Creator. As with St. Brendan, the songs of the birds can also bring our thoughts to God.

St. Francis of Assisi also had a wonderful encounter with birds that is recorded in *The Little Flowers of Saint Francis of Assisi*. One day, while walking along, Francis came to a tree full of many birds. He told his fellow friars to "wait for me here, while I go and preach to my little sisters the birds." Francis approached the tree, and the birds gathered around and listened intently until Francis blessed them to leave. One of the friars, Brother James of Massa, reported what Francis preached to the birds that day:

My little sisters the birds, you owe much to God, your Creator, and ought to sing His praise at all times and in all places, because He has given you liberty and the air to fly about in; and though you neither spin nor sew, He has given you a twofold and threefold clothing for yourselves and your offspring; and He sent two of your species into the Ark with Noah that you might not be lost to the world; besides which, He feeds you, though you neither sow nor reap. He has given you fountains and rivers to quench your thirst, mountains and valleys in which to take refuge, and trees in which to build your nests; so that your Creator loves you much, having thus favored you with such bounties. Beware, my little sisters, of the sin of ingratitude, and study always to praise the Lord.

It is written that the birds, after hearing these words from the holy saint, "began to open their beaks, stretch their necks, flap their wings, and to bow their heads to the ground" to show their joy to Francis for his wonderful message.[123]

The birds in this story were a reminder to St. Francis of Christ. We all could benefit from this sermon to the birds if we pictured in our mind Francis talking to us instead of to the birds. God has given us so many things in his creation to be thankful for, and that should cause us, like the birds, to open our mouths, stretch our necks, and shout to God for joy!

Another story that involves our feathered friends in the history of Catholic saints centers around St. Benedict of Nursia, the sixth-century Italian who is considered the father of Western monasticism because he is the founder of the Benedictine Order.

Jealous of Benedict's holy virtue and the fame his monasteries were gaining, a local priest one day tried to kill Benedict. To do this, he poisoned a loaf of bread and sent it to Benedict as a present. Benedict, through knowledge given to him by the Holy Spirit, knew that the loaf was poisoned but still gladly received it as a gift from the priest.

Thankfully, there was a raven that daily came and visited Benedict from the local woods, and Benedict would give it bread to eat. When the raven came to Benedict on this day, Benedict looked at the raven and said to the bird, "In the name of Jesus Christ our Lord, take up that loaf, and leave it in some such place where no man may find it."[124] The raven obeyed and took the bread far from that place where it was never seen again. For this reason, Benedict is often portrayed in Christian art with a raven.

This story shows how birds can develop friendships with humans and even look out for us when we are in danger. St. Benedict and the Raven demonstrates a perfect example of living the Golden Rule from Matthew 7:12, "Do to others whatever you would have them do to you." Benedict is kind to the bird, and in turn, the bird is kind to Benedict.

Finally, St. Kevin of Glendalough, a sixth-century Irish saint, also has a delightful tale associated with birds that points our gaze to God and the virtue of patience. Legends say that Kevin was one day deep in prayer with his arms outstretched in the form of a cross. While he was praying, a blackbird came and built a nest in his hands and laid her eggs there. Kevin is said to have remained in that position until the eggs hatched.[125]

It is sometimes difficult for us to comprehend and even believe these miraculous stories that come down to us through the ages. We are not required to believe them; however, God uses birds to direct our gaze to the holy, and just because something may seem impossible to us, that does not mean that it is impossible to God. After all, Jesus rose from the dead.

BUGGING OUT

"These tiny ants have proceeded from his thought just as much as I. It caused him just as much trouble to create the angels as these animals and the flowers on the trees."
—St. Catherine of Siena

I n my first fifteen years of teaching, I have been able to notice, observe, and learn one thing that is constantly changing and growing in the great field of education: acronyms. There are so many of them in the everyday life of a teacher that my head is left spinning and I feel that I could just LOL or ROFL. In fact, I am quite sure that sometimes educators are just making up acronyms to sound as if they know what they are talking about in meetings and professional development.

I come into contact with so many acronyms on a regular basis—such as ACT, IEP, SAT—that they exhaust me. After most meetings, I come away thinking that I have just been in a two-hour episode of Sesame Street or Baby Einstein that was sponsored by the uppercase letters ADD.

There is little I can do about this educational trend but to endure it and move on to the next acronym that will rear its consonant-ladened head. Acronyms have taught me to accept some things at my workplace that I am unable to change, but they do not make me cringe nearly as much as the fact that we are constantly encompassed at all times by insects and bugs!

The Smithsonian Institute estimates there are approximately 900,000 species of insects currently accounted for on earth. However, scientists estimate there could be up to 30 million total that are undiscovered in hard-to-reach places. Also, at any given time, there are some 10 quintillion (10,000,000,000,000,000,000) individual insects alive.[126] Take that in for a moment.

If you have a fear of bugs and the creepy-crawly things of this world, those numbers are truly unsettling. We are living on a planet inhabited in every corner by bugs. As with the acronyms at my workplace, there is no way to avoid coming into daily contact with them. This fact is true not only for us, but also in Scripture and in the lives of the saints.

Bugs in the Bible

Insects not only surround us in our everyday lives, but they also inundate the Bible, and their symbolism is often that of an awful pest, or one considered to be a great symbol of hope.

For instance, insects were one of the main plagues God used in freeing the Israelites from the yoke of slavery placed on them by the Egyptians. Three of the ten plagues the Egyptians endured because of the hardness of Pharaoh's heart were insect related, and just reading the accounts can have us scratching our skin and looking for the bug repellant.

The third plague God placed upon the Egyptians in Exodus 8:12–15 was the plague of the gnats.

The Lord spoke to Moses: Speak to Aaron: Stretch
out your staff and strike the dust of the earth, and
it will turn into gnats throughout the land of Egypt.
They did so. Aaron stretched out his hand with his
staff and struck the dust of the earth, and gnats came
upon human being and beast alike. All the dust of
the earth turned into gnats throughout the land of
Egypt. Though the magicians did the same thing to
produce gnats by their magic arts, they could not do
so. The gnats were on human being and beast alike,
and the magicians said to Pharaoh, "This is the finger
of God." Yet Pharaoh hardened his heart and would
not listen to them, just as the Lord had said.

John F. Craghan points out: "Unlike the first two plagues,
this plague is one which the Egyptian magicians are incapable
of reproducing. In the magicians' report to Pharaoh there is the
further observation: 'This is the finger of God.'"[127] By being unable
to summon a plague of gnats, they begin to see their strength is
failing and they are no match for the power of God.

This plague seems absolutely horrific because of my own
experiences with gnats. In Arkansas, we have a gnat called the
Buffalo Gnat. Thankfully, these creatures are not the size of
buffalo, but they are awful pests. To summarize, a Buffalo Gnat
is a blood-sucking fly that causes symptoms similar to those of
mosquito bites. However, they are even more dangerous to
other animals, as the University of Illinois College of Veterinary
Medicine points out: "Livestock and poultry are sometimes killed
by the flies when bitten by large numbers of them. Death can be
due to anaphylactic shock, toxemia, blood loss, or suffocation when
the flies are inhaled."[128] Every year, around the end of March,
these gnats hatch and can be found all over the state of Arkansas.

They get so annoying that some people would rather stay inside on a beautiful spring day than go outside. That annoyance for the Egyptians, coupled with what is probably the loss of many livestock and chickens, does not soften Pharaoh's heart. As a result, another plague is placed upon the Egyptians, and this one also involves insects.

The fourth plague of the Egyptians was the plague of flies. Exodus 8:17–20 details this horrible plague God placed on the people of Egypt in order to free the Israelites from slavery.

> For if you do not let my people go, I will send swarms of flies upon you and your servants and your people and your houses. The houses of the Egyptians and the very ground on which they stand will be filled with swarms of flies. But on that day I will make an exception of the land of Goshen, where my people are, and no swarms of flies will be there, so that you may know that I the Lord am in the midst of the land. I will make a distinction between my people and your people. This sign will take place tomorrow. This the Lord did. Thick swarms of flies entered the house of Pharaoh and the houses of his servants; throughout Egypt the land was devastated on account of the swarms of flies.

In the Bible, flies often bring evil. In Christianity, they also often represent sin, which goes hand and hand with evil.[129]

I grew up on a small cattle farm in the Arkansas River Valley. Sometimes, when I was out in a pasture, feeding cattle or cutting hay, I would come across an animal carcass. The carcass was always swarming with flies. As I reflect on those dead animals, and the fourth plague of the Egyptians, I can see the flies swarming the Egyptian homes as a symbol of their oncoming death: death because of Pharaoh's sin and as a reminder to us that all sin leads to death.

Exodus 10:12–15 chronicles the eighth plague, that of locusts or grasshoppers:

> The LORD then said to Moses: Stretch out your hand over the land of Egypt for the locusts, that they may come upon it and eat up all the land's vegetation, whatever the hail has left. So Moses stretched out his staff over the land of Egypt, and the LORD drove an east wind over the land all that day and all night. When it was morning, the east wind brought the locusts. The locusts came up over the whole land of Egypt and settled down over all its territory. Never before had there been such a fierce swarm of locusts, nor will there ever be again. They covered the surface of the whole land, so that it became black. They ate up all the vegetation in the land and all the fruit of the trees the hail had spared. Nothing green was left on any tree or plant in the fields throughout the land of Egypt.

Grasshoppers don't seem all that bad when compared with the other insect plagues. However, grasshoppers are different from most insects because they devour great quantities of food in every stage of their lifecycle. In fact, they can eat up to sixteen times their own body weight per day.[130] With that kind of appetite, and covering the land of Egypt, they must have caused death and destruction all over by wiping out all of the vegetation in the area. The food chain would have been destroyed, leading to the decimation of the animal population as well as the death of many Egyptian people.

But at the far end of the exodus from slavery in Egypt comes the Promised Land, and there we see the only real hope for insects in the Scriptures, where they are not considered a pest or a plague. There, we have at least the foretaste of the mighty bee.

Bees, not physically but figuratively, lead the Israelites to the Promised Land in Exodus 3:8. After all, the Promised Land is described as a wonderful place "flowing with milk and honey." The reason that this place in the land of Israel is flowing with honey is, according to those who really know, because "Its dry climate, its rich abundance, and its variety of aromatic flowers, and its limestone rocks render it particularly adapted for bees."[131]

Throughout salvation history, the bee has also been a symbol of regal or kingly power.[132] Because of this, when the Israelites travel to the Promised Land "flowing with milk and honey," the presence of honey in the passage shows us that they are truly going to the place of the king, which for a time will be earthly kings, but later will become the home of the true king, Jesus.

Bugs in the Lives of Saints

If insects are usually seen as pests in Scripture, they are portrayed even worse in the records of church history. For example, fifteenth-century St. Catherine of Genoa went to Confession one day and fell into ecstasy. She was shown many things by the Holy Spirit in this vision and she was never the same again. After the vision, Catherine gave herself to the care of patients in the hospital of Genoa. One story tells of her so overcome with love for her patients that she is said to have eaten the lice and scabies-causing mites that infested them so that they would be more comfortable in their stay and might heal more quickly.

When I first read this story, I could not believe it. In fact, I had to check multiple sources before I would actually believe this happened. Why on earth would anyone eat the lice and mites on their hospital patients? To understand how the lice and mites helped St. Catherine draw closer to God, it is first helpful to understand why some saints undertook extreme mortifications as Catherine did. Reflecting on this, St. Alphonsus Ligouri explains, "To preserve her soul and body free from stain, she must also chastise her flesh, by fasting, abstinence, by disciplines and other penitential works. And if she has not health or strength to practice such mortifications, she ought at least to bear in peace her infirmities and pains, and to accept cheerfully the contempt and ill-treatment that she receives from others." He adds that mortifications are necessary to "restrain the inordinate inclinations of self-love."[133]

Eating those disgusting insects was a way for St. Catherine to express her total abandonment of love of herself in favor of the love of Christ and her neighbor. This grotesque and macabre mortification showed that there was no length to which she would not go to live her faith and love God.

Two other saints also used insects to lessen their love of self and increase their love for Christ. St. Ite of Killedy, a sixth-century Irish saint known for her lengthy fasts and strange asceticism, would let a stag beetle, a beetle with huge front mandibles, eat away at the flesh of the side of her body as a way to repent of her sins.[134] I think I'll leave that one there.

Then there was St. Macarius the Great, a very holy fourth-century Egyptian hermit who lived in the wilds of Egypt. It is said that one day he inadvertently killed a gnat that had bitten him on the arm. He felt so much remorse for this action that he went to live in a mosquito-infested swamp for six months. When he returned from the swamp, his body was covered in bites and sores.[135]

St. Catherine, St. Macarius, and St. Ite all saw insects as a way to draw closer to God and die to self. These mortifications seem strange and extreme to us today, especially when some of our biggest sacrifices may only be giving up chocolate for Lent or meat on Fridays. However, our little sacrifices can be a reminder of the tiny insects in the stories of these saints. They may be small, unnoticeable at times, and annoying, but they can also help us grow in love of Christ and our neighbor.

On a personal note, I can relate to St. Macarius the Great becoming distraught at killing an insect. Though not going to the extent of living in a swamp for six months, I still try not to kill insects if I can help it. When one crawls, slithers, or flies into my home, I try to pick it up and place it outside. Even the tiniest creation like this is special to God, and though sometimes I end up squashing one or breaking its leg in the process of relocation, I still try to save them. I believe if God can love someone as small and insignificant as me, I can give that tiny life another shot at the outdoors.

Thankfully, there are some more wholesome stories with insects in the lives of the saints, and similar to those in the Bible, they mostly involve bees. For instance, when St. Ambrose was an infant he was found with his face covered in bees. Tradition holds that this was a sign that the future saint would be "honey-tongued" for the rest of his life, and a great speaker. These prophetic words must have been true, as he was responsible for helping to convert one of the greatest Catholic thinkers in history, St. Augustine of Hippo. And because of his honey-tongued incident with the bees, Ambrose is now the patron saint of beekeepers.[136]

Another bee tale involving an infant and their future is St. Rita of Cascia. It is said that when Rita was five days old, on the day after her Baptism, a swarm of bees landed on her face while she was sleeping in her cradle. The bees entered and left her mouth without causing any harm. They were a foreshadowing of the sweet and kind person she would be in her life.[137]

These stories call to mind another representation of bees in Christianity—that of being tireless workers. In order to be saints, St. Ambrose and St. Rita worked tirelessly, like bees, to live a holy life and bring others to the faith. Next time we see a bee flying around a flower bed during summertime, may they be a reminder to us that we also need to work tirelessly to bring ourselves and others closer to Christ.

Finally, I have one story involving a spider, and I believe it is a story worth telling. In third-century Rome, Christians were being hunted down and killed due to their persecution by the Emperor Decius. Two of these Christians, St. Felix of Nola and St. Maximus, were being chased by Roman soldiers. It is said that the two ran into a vacant building to hide. Once they were inside the building, a spider quickly spun a web over the door to make it appear long abandoned before the soldiers arrived. The soldiers passed by the two saints, and the two fugitives survived.[138]

This story reminds me so much of how I sometimes pass by the poor and homeless without giving them a second thought. Like the soldiers, I pass them by as if a spider web is covering their face, hiding the saint that may lie underneath. I hope that I can learn to look past the cobwebs and see what truly lies inside that person. We all have webs that cover up parts of our heart and soul. We need someone to help us take down those webs to uncover the gifts that we all have to help build up the Church. In the third century, a spider web saved two saints' lives. They lived longer in order to do great things for the kingdom of God. In this century, taking down the webs may be what we need most to save others.

In closing, insects provide us with some truly gross stories. But they also can teach us many things about our faith. We need to be hardworking like the honeybee. We need to abandon love of self like some of those saints who used insects as an extreme form of penance. Finally, we need to stay faithful to God and not harden our hearts toward him as Pharaoh did in the bug-related plagues of Egypt. Insects surround us, just as the love of God surrounds each of us.

GOAT

"Greatest of all time."

I n the world of social media, texting, and cyberspace, when you write the word *goat*, people no longer think of that cute creature with rectangular pupils that will eat anything while getting its head stuck in fences. Nowadays, the word "goat" calls to mind the acronym GOAT, which stands for the Greatest of All Time. This acronym has brought forth a barrage of senseless and useless bickering that will never truly have an outcome or answer.

Sports talk shows are constantly yelling and screaming about who is the GOAT in the National Basketball Association, or NBA. Is it Michael Jordan, Lebron James, Magic Johnson, Shaq, Kobe, Kareem, or Wilt? The same conversation then turns to the National Football League (NFL). Who is the GOAT at the quarterback position? Tom Brady, Peyton Manning, Joe Montana, or John Elway? Maybe I left out a person on that list that you think is better, and therefore you want to argue with me now.

Sports are not the only place we argue about GOATs. Musicians, writers, actors, actresses, presidents, vice presidents, restaurants, and basically anything else that a person can have an opinion on can be turned into a roaring GOAT debate. Even the Catholic Church has GOAT debates. Who is the GOAT saint or the GOAT pope? The endless cacophony leaves me weary and longing for the day when a goat was simply a goat.

In Genesis chapter 37, the story of Jacob's youngest son Joseph is told, and a goat is part of that story. Jacob had twelve sons! Today, that would probably warrant a reality show on a second-tier TV network about the family's struggles and the strife of living together in such a large group.

One of those episodes' plots would probably go something like this: Jacob, father of twelve boys, loved the youngest son Joseph the most. The other brothers got jealous of Joseph because of his dad's love for him, so they decided to kill him. The brothers, however, did not kill him. Instead, they threw him in a well and took away his coat. They returned home, found a goat, killed it, and dipped Joseph's coat in the goat's blood. Then they reported that Joseph had been killed by a wild beast. That sounds like a TV show I would watch!

A word we use today, "scapegoat" (meaning, one that bears the blame for others), comes to my mind when I hear the story of Joseph and his brethren. Joseph was being blamed for being his father's favorite. The goat's blood in the story takes the place of Joseph's blood. If goats can bear the blame for others and shed their blood for us, I am thankful that Jesus was the GOAT that bore the blame for me and all of us. No debate is necessary.

I always dreamed while growing up of being a veterinarian so I could help animals. Somewhere along the road of life, I woke up from that dream and went in pursuit of other interests. I'm a math teacher instead, and that's just fine with me. However, my love for animals remains, and I hope that this small work may kindle in your heart a new appreciation for God's furry friends and creation, too. God bless you, and thank you for reading!

ACKNOWLEDGMENTS

There are so many wonderful people that I wish to thank for helping this work come to fruition. First, to my wife, Christy, thank you so much for being my first reader and listening to my ideas as they came out of my head. Thank you to Jon Sweeney and Paraclete Press for taking a chance on me and my first published work. Thank you to Sara Putman for helping me find my writing voice through all her critiques and suggestions. Thank you to Deacon Dr. Paul Cronan, Ben Rowse, and Catherine Upchurch for also critiquing my writing and giving me ideas on how to improve it. Also, thank you to my family and friends for supporting me in this endeavor, and a special thanks to Sherry Siler for helping me with marketing ideas for the book. Finally, I would like to thank the animals. Without them, there would be a lot less beauty in our world and a lot less fun.

NOTES

CHAPTER 1

1 *brings down those perceived to be mighty:* Pauly Fongemie, "Signs: Animals," Catholictradition .org. Accessed September 17, 2020 at http://www.catholictradition.org/Saints/signs1.htm.

2 *When Samson sees the Philistines:* John A Grindel, *The Collegeville Bible Commentary: Based on the New American Bible* (Collegeville, MN: Liturgical Press, 1992), 261.

3 *A donkey's jawbone is only about nine inches in length:* John McArthur, "Samson: Playing with Fire and Getting Burned," Grace to You, September 10, 2015. Accessed September 17, 2020 at https://www.gty.org/library/blog/B150910/samson-playing-with-fire-and-getting-burned.

4 *'meek' in his corresponding role as servant:* Mary Margaret Pazdan, *The Collegeville Bible Commentary*, 618.

5 *honored by Christ, tradition says:* Peter Klein, *The Catholic Source Book* (Dubuque, IA: Harcourt Religion Publishers, 2000), 469.

6 *There is a famous story involving him and a mule:* "Finding St. Anthony: His Art and Miracles," Franciscan Media, May 25, 2011. Accessed September 17, 2020 at https://www.franciscanmedia .org/finding-st-anthony-his-art-and-miracles/.

7 *Anthony held the host in front of the mule:* Charles Warren Stoddard, *Saint Anthony: The Wonder Worker of Padua* (Rockford, IL: Tan Books, 1978), 66–67.

8 *Guillard was humbled by God's grace and made good on his promise:* Stoddard, *Saint Anthony*, 66–67.

9 *there is a beautiful Renaissance-era painting by Domenico Beccafumi:* Domenico Beccafumi, *Saint Anthony and the Miracle of the Mule*, 1537. Accessed September 17, 2020 at https:// commons.wikimedia.org/wiki/Category:Saint_Anthony_and_the_Miracle_of_the_Mule_-_ Domenico_Beccafumi_-_Louvre_RF_1966-2.

10 *his donkey wept for him:* "St Francis and the Animals," MonasteryIcons.com. Accessed September 17, 2020 at https://www.monasteryicons.com/product/Saint-Francis-and-the-Animals/did-you-know.

11 *being a careful and considerate handler is vital:* "Understanding Donkey Characteristics," TheDonkeySanctuary.org.uk. Accessed September 17, 2020 at https://www.thedonkeysanctuary .org.uk/what-we-do/knowledge-and-advice/for-owners/understanding-donkey-characteristics.

12 *giving our friend the donkey a special place in Church tradition:* Maria Augusta Von Trapp, "The Tradition of the Christmas Crèche," CatholicExchange.com. December 11, 2018. Accessed September 17, 2020 at https://catholicexchange.com/the-tradition-of-the-christmas-creche.

13 *the song tells the story of a donkey that helps Santa Claus:* "Dominick the Italian Christmas Donkey: Story, Words and Music," Explore-Italian-Culture.com. Accessed September 17, 2020 at https://www.explore-italian-culture.com/italian-christmas-donkey.html.

CHAPTER 2

14 *there really is not a specific reason given that God would forbid some meats and not others:* Wayne A. Turner, *The Collegeville Bible Commentary: Based on the New American Bible* (Collegeville, MN: Liturgical Press, 1992), 127.

15 *These restrictions apply to people in everyday life:* Lawrence Boadt, *Reading the Old Testament: An Introduction.* New York: Paulist Press, 1984, 189.

16 *External things, like the food one eats, do not make a person evil:* Philip Van Linden, *The Collegeville Bible Commentary*, 917–918.

17 *All nations and people are invited to the banquet:* Van Linden, *The Collegeville Bible Commentary*, 914.

18 *the rite of blessing of throats is now carried out with two wax candles:* Joseph Pronechen, "How St. Blaise Saved a City and More Fascinating Facts About Him," *National Catholic Register*, February 3, 2020. Accessed September 17, 2020 at http://www.ncregister.com/blog/joseph -pronechen/st-blaise-saves-a-city-and-more-fascinating-little-known-facts-about-him.

19   *may God deliver you from every disease of the throat:* "Blessing of Throats," Liturgies.net. Accessed September 17, 2020 at http://www.liturgies.net/saints/blaise/blessingofthroats.htm.

20   *St. Brigid then cared for the boar and released it into her own herd:* "Brigid of Kildare: A Saint or the Goddess of Spring?" *The Irish News,* January 30, 2016. Accessed September 17, 2020 at http://www.irishnews.com/lifestyle/2016/01/30/news/brigid-of-kildare-a-saint-of-the-goddess-of-spring--395161/.

21   *Juniper is said to have prepared the pig's foot with great love and kindness:* Henry Edward Manning, *The Little Flowers of Saint Francis of Assisi* (Old Saybrook, CT: Konecky & Konecky, 1915), 215–218.

22   *Pig farmers would see Anthony and a pig together in a painting or a statue:* "Saint Anthony the Abbot," CatholicSaints.Info. January 29, 2019. Accessed September 17, 2020 at https://catholicsaints.info/saint-anthony-the-abbot/.

23   *Chesterton had the following to say:* G. K. Chesterton, "Rhapsody on a Pig," *G. K. Weekly.* October 21, 2009. Accessed September 17, 2020 at https://chesterton.wordpress.com/2009/10/21/rhapsody-on-a-pig/.

CHAPTER 3

24   *they follow a leader who even eats the flesh of pigs and rats:* The Father William Most Theological Collection, "Commentary on the Old Testament Prophets: Isaiah," CatholicCulture.org. Accessed September 17, 2020 at https://www.catholicculture.org/culture/library/most/getwork.cfm?worknum=93.

25   *The Philistines know enough Israelite history:* Paula J. Bowes, *The Collegeville Bible Commentary,* 270.

26   *The farmer was overcome with joy at the miracle:* Eduard Saint-Omer, *St. Gerard Majella: The Wonder-worker and Patron of Expectant Mothers* (Rockford, IL: Tan Books, 1999), 150–151.

27   *By Your power may these injurious animals be driven off:* "Prayer Against Pests," Catholic.org. Accessed September 17, 2020 at https://www.catholic.org/prayers/prayer.php?p=1708.

28   *The little mouse scampered hesitantly to the food bowl and ate peacefully:* Alex Garcia-Rivera, "Come Together: St. Martin De Porres," USCatholic.org. Accessed September 17, 2020 at https://www.uscatholic.org/church/2010/06/come-together-st-martin-de-porres.

CHAPTER 4

29   *Water as a source of life and death is a common biblical image:* Irene Nowell, *The Collegeville Bible Commentary,* 837.

30   *the image of the all-powerful Creator:* Nowell, *The Collegeville Bible Commentary,* 829.

31   *The Eucharist is 'the source and summit of the Christian life':* Catechism of the Catholic Church, "The sacrament of the Eucharist." Accessed September 17, 2020 at https://www.vatican.va/archive/ccc_css/archive/catechism/p2s2c1a3.htm.

32   *The feeding was viewed as an anticipation or preview of the Last Supper:* Daniel J. Harrington, SJ, *The Collegeville Bible Commentary,* 883.

33   *its letters were an acronym for "Jesus Christ, Son of God, Savior":* Peter Klein, *The Catholic Source Book.* Dubuque, IA: Harcourt Religion, 2000, 192. And "Symbolism of the Fish," Catholic.org. Accessed September 17, 2020 at https://www.catholic.org/encyclopedia/view.php?id=6017.

34   *the Ichthys became a covert sign to identify their beliefs:* Philip Kosloski, "Why Do Christians Use the Fish Symbol?" Aleteia.org, May 22, 2017. Accessed September 17, 2020 at https://aleteia.org/2017/05/22/why-do-christians-use-the-fish-symbol/.

35   *fish were responsible for saving several Eucharistic hosts:* "Eucharistic Miracle of Alboraya-Almacera," TheRealPresence.org. Accessed September 17, 2020 at http://www.therealpresence.org/eucharst/mir/english_pdf/Alboraya1.pdf.

36   *My brothers the fish:* Stoddard, *Saint Anthony,* 61–63.

37 *Why do Catholics not eat meat on Friday?*: Eleonore Villarrubia, "Why Do Catholics Eat Fish on Friday?" Catholicism.org. February 16, 2010. Accessed September 17, 2020 at https://catholicism.org/why-do-catholics-eat-fish-on-friday-2.html.

38 *Abstinence from meat on Fridays led McDonald's to create the Filet-O-Fish sandwich:* "Filet-O-Fish Tale," originally in The Cincinnati Enquirer, February 26, 2007, accessed at the Chicago Tribune on September 17, 2020: https://www.chicagotribune.com/news/ct-xpm-2007-02-26-0702260163-story.html.

CHAPTER 5

39 *this "word is translated sometimes in our Douay-Rheims by rhinoceros:* "Animals in the Bible," Catholic Encyclopedia, NewAdvent.org. Accessed September 17, 2020 at http://www.newadvent.org/cathen/01517a.htm.

40 *Basilisk (basiliscus) is a Greek word:* Philip Kosloski, "The Biblical and Christian Roots of the Basilisk," Aleteia.org, July 31, 2017. Accessed September 17, 2020 at https://aleteia.org/2017/07/31/the-biblical-and-christian-roots-of-the-basilisk/.

41 *as an equivalent for several Hebrew names of snakes:* "Animals in the Bible," NewAdvent.org.

42 *Some scholars conjecture:* USCCB, "Scripture." Accessed September 17, 2020 at http://www.usccb.org/bible/job/40.

43 *the two beasts are meant as symbols:* Michael D. Guinan, The Collegeville Bible Commentary, 697.

44 *Columba is said to have made the sign of the cross in front of the monster:* Angelo Stagnaro, "St. Columba and the Loch Ness Monster," National Catholic Register. Accessed September 17, 2020 at http://www.ncregister.com/blog/astagnaro/st.-columba-and-the-loch-ness-monster. And The Editors, "Loch Ness Monster," History.com, October 06, 2017. Accessed September 17, 2020 at https://www.history.com/topics/folklore/loch-ness-monster.

45 *St. George appeared before the beast:* "St. George – Saints & Angels," Catholic.org. Accessed September 17, 2020 at https://www.catholic.org/saints/saint.php?saint_id=280.

46 *"How Gargoyles Save Souls...and Ceilings":* Daniel Espara, "How Gargoyles save Souls...and Ceilings," CatholicEducation.org. Accessed September 17, 2020 at https://www.catholiceducation.org/en/culture/art/how-gargoyles-save-souls-and-ceilings.html.

CHAPTER 6

47 *that cow will produce five hundred more pints of milk a year:* Caroline Gammell, "Cows with Names Produce More Milk, Scientists Say," The Telegraph, TheTelegraph.co.uk, January 28, 2009. Accessed September 17, 2020 at https://www.telegraph.co.uk/news/earth/agriculture/farming/4358115/Cows-with-names-produce-more-milk-scientists-say.html.

48 *a group of dairy farmers noticed their cows had different moos:* Melissa Breyer, "21 Things You Didn't Know about Cows," Mother Nature Network, March 12, 2018. Accessed September 17, 2020 at https://www.mnn.com/earth-matters/animals/stories/20-things-you-didnt-know-about-cows.

49 *Cows in Sacred Scripture have historically stood for patience:* Pauly Fongemie, "Signs: Animals," CatholicTradition.org.

50 *Joseph follows his interpretation with practical advice:* Pauline Viviano, The Collegeville Bible Commentary, 73.

51 *they saw the bull as a symbol of strength and vitality:* USCCB, Accessed September 17, 2020 at http://www.usccb.org/bible/exodus/32.

52 *A parable this rich blossoms out with new meaning:* Jerome Kodell, The Collegeville Bible Commentary, 965.

53 *his buddies in school nicknamed him "Dumb Ox":* Deacon Keith Fournier, "St. Thomas Aquinas, a Corpulent Man Nicknamed the Dumb Ox Shows Us How to Live for Jesus," Catholic News Agency. Accessed September 17, 2020 at https://www.catholicnewsagency.com/column/st-thomas-aquinas-a-corpulent-man-nicknamed-the-dumb-ox-shows-us-how-to-live-for-jesus-3437.

54 *his bellowings will fill the world:* G. K. Chesterton, *Saint Thomas Aquinas: The Dumb Ox* (Nashville, TN: Sam Torode Book Arts, 2010), 33–34.

55 *the cow was able to produce milk ten times the normal amount:* Whitney Hopler, "Who Was Saint Brigid?" Thoughtco, August 12, 2018. Accessed September 17, 2020 at https://www.thoughtco .com/who-was-saint-brigid-124534.

56 *O Lord, deal not with us according to our sins:* "Blessing of Diseased Cattle – Prayers," Catholic. org. Accessed September 17, 2020 at https://www.catholic.org/prayers/prayer .php?p=380.

CHAPTER 7

57 *Commentators in the Ignatius Catholic Study Bible point out:* Scott Hahn, Curtis Mitch, and Dennis Walters, *Genesis: With Introduction, Commentary, and Notes* (San Francisco: Ignatius Press, 2010), Kindle Edition, location 4115-4119.

58 *The paschal lamb prefigured Jesus Christ:* George Leo Haydock, "Commentary on Exodus 12:4," George Haydock's Catholic Bible Commentary. Accessed September 17, 2020 at https://www .studylight.org/commentaries/hcc/exodus-12.html.

59 *After agreeing to baptize him along with the sinners:* Catechism of the Catholic Church, "Jesus Died Crucified." Accessed September 17, 2020 at https://www.vatican.va/archive/ccc_css/archive/ catechism/p122a4p2.htm.

60 *According to the doctrine of the Catholic Church:* "Apparitions and Appearances – Mary, Mother of God," Catholic.org. Accessed September 17, 2020 at https://www.catholic.org/mary/appear. php.

61 *fifteen people in Knock, Ireland, witnessed an apparition of Mary:* "History Explore the History of Knock Shrine," KnockShrine.ie. Accessed September 17, 2020 at https://www.knockshrine.ie/ history/. And Father James, OFM Cap, "The Story of Knock." Accessed September 17, 2020 at https://www.ewtn.com/catholicism/library/story-of-knock-5600.

62 *Ignorance of the Scriptures is ignorance of Christ:* Philip Kosloski, "10 Witty Quotes from Saint Jerome," Aleteia, June 7, 2017. Accessed September 17, 2020 at https://aleteia.org/2016/09/30/10 -witty-quotes-from-saint-jerome/.

63 *A sixteenth-century figure, St. Germaine Cousin:* "St. Germaine Cousin – Saints & Angels," Catholic. org. Accessed September 17, 2020 at https://www.catholic.org/saints/saint.php?saint_id=52.

64 *Clement saw a lamb scraping at the soil with one of its feet:* "Pope St. Clement I – Saints & Angels," Catholic.org. Accessed September 17, 2020 at https://www.catholic.org/saints/saint .php?saint_id=37.

CHAPTER 8

65 *people who own a cat are 40 percent less likely to die of a heart attack:* Purina, "How Can Cats Reduce Stress and Improve Moods?" Purina.com. Accessed September 17, 2020 at https://www .purina.com/articles/cat/getting-a-cat/how-can-cats-improve-moods-and-reduce-stress

66 *they are capable of purring at a vibration between 25 to 150 Hertz:* Amy Kuras, "101 Amazing Cat Facts: Fun Trivia About Your Feline Friend," Care.com. Accessed September 17, 2020 at https://www .care.com/c/stories/6045/101-amazing-cat-facts-fun-trivia-about-your-feline-friend/.

67 *Mary Todd Lincoln was once asked what her husband Abraham Lincoln's hobby was:* National Parks Service, "Lincoln Pets." Accessed September 17, 2020 at https://www.nps.gov/abli/ planyourvisit/lincoln-pets.htm.

68 *the lion is known "as the classical symbol of strength:* "Animals in the Bible," NewAdvent.org.

69 *It is the spirit of the Lord that gives Samson the strength:* John A. Grindel, *The Collegeville Bible Commentary*, 260.

70 *A satrap was a local governor:* Merriam-Webster, "Satrap." Accessed September 17, 2020 at https://www.merriam-webster.com/dictionary/satrap.

71 *A lion has the tenth most powerful bite in the world:* The Mysterious World, "Top 10 Most Powerful Animal Bites." Accessed September 17, 2020 at https://themysteriousworld.com/most-powerful-animal-bites/.

72 *The 'God of all grace' wants us to be happy:* Jerome H. Neyrey, *The Collegeville Bible Commentary: New Testament / Based on the New American Bible.* Collegeville, MN: Liturgical Press, 1992, 1234.

73 *Blessed Maria Bagnesi was a very holy sixteenth-century Dominican tertiary:* CatholicSaints. Info, "Blessed Maria Bagnesi," February 01, 2019. Accessed September 17, 2020 at https://catholicsaints.info/blessed-maria-bagnesi/.

74 *Cats that live in the wild or indoor pets allowed to roam outdoors:* Chuck Raasch, "Cats Kill up to 3.7B Birds Annually," *USA Today,* January 30, 2013. Accessed September 17, 2020 at https://www.usatoday.com/story/news/nation/2013/01/29/cats-wild-birds-mammals-study/1873871/.

75 *St. Gertrude of Nivelles was a seventh-century Benedictine saint:* Catholic Library, "St. Gertrude of Nivelles," NewAdvent.org. Accessed September 17, 2020 at http://www.newadvent.org/cathen/06533c.htm. And Thomas J. Craughwell, *Heaven Help Us: 300 Patron Saints to Call upon for Every Occasion* (New York: Chartwell Books, 2016), 105.

76 *Cats tend to hide their illnesses:* "How to Tell If Your Cat Is Sick or in Pain." Vetstreet.com, January 30, 2015. Accessed September 17, 2020 at http://www.vetstreet.com/our-pet-experts/how-to-tell-if-your-cat-is-sick-7-symptoms-to-watch-out-for.

77 *Lions are highly territorial:* College of Biological Sciences, "Social Behavior: Group Living." Accessed September 17, 2020 at https://cbs.umn.edu/research/labs/packer/social-behavior#:~:text=Lions%20are%20highly%20territorial%20and,to%20water%20and%20denning%20sites.

CHAPTER 9

78 *[snakes] have been a symbol for Satan and evil:* Pauly Fongemie, "Signs: Animals," CatholicTradition. org.

79 *In Canaan the serpent was associated with the fertility cults:* Pauline Viviano, *The Collegeville Bible Commentary,* 43.

80 *The healing of the bites is linked to obedience and to faith:* Helen Kenik Mainelli, *The Collegeville Bible Commentary,* 178.

81 *What makes such bold and unrelenting prayer possible:* Pablo T. Gadenz, *The Gospel of Luke* (Grand Rapids, MI: Baker Academic, 2018), 224.

82 *Pheme Perkins comments:* Pheme Perkins, *The Collegeville Bible Commentary,* 1286.

83 *The church's missionaries had nothing to fear:* Philip Van Linden, *The Collegeville Bible Commentary,* 934–935.

84 *Mark 16.18 does not say that Christians should catch poisonous snakes:* Brantly Millegan, "Why Don't Catholics Practice Snake-Handling?" Aleteia, February 17, 2014. Accessed September 17, 2020 at https://aleteia.org/2014/02/17/why-dont-catholics-practice-snake-handling/.

85 *St. Patrick was once attacked by snakes:* Philip Kosloski, "Did St. Patrick Expel Snakes from Ireland?" Aleteia, March 16, 2018. Accessed September 17, 2020 at https://aleteia.org/2018/03/16/did-st-patrick-expel-snakes-from-ireland/.

86 *This dream meant that the rope was a symbol for the rosary:* Brian Kranick, "The Snake and the Rosary: The Dreams of St. John Bosco," *Catholic Exchange,* February 02, 2018. Accessed September 17, 2020 at https://catholicexchange.com/snake-rosary-dreams-st-john-bosco.

87 *she was removed from the viper pit completely unharmed:* St. Irene Byzantine Catholic Church, website, saintirene.org. Accessed September 17, 2020.

88 *Every year, on the Greek island of Kefalonia:* "Holy Snakes! A Marian Feast Day's Strange, Stunning Miracle," Catholic News Agency. August 15, 2018. Accessed September 17, 2020 at https://www.catholicnewsagency.com/news/holy-snakes-a-marian-feast-days-strange-stunning-miracle-12114.

CHAPTER 10

89 *Women have love affairs with horses:* Lucy Cavendish, "Why We Love Horses," *The Guardian*, November 5, 2005. Accessed September 17, 2020 at https://www.theguardian.com/uk/2005/nov/06/gender.world.

90 *What is it with women and horses?:* Molly Watson, "The Lure of the Saddle," *The Spectator*, May 23, 2018. Accessed September 17, 2020 at https://www.spectator.co.uk/2018/05/why-are-so-many-women-obsessed-with-horses/.

91 *the horse is mentioned in relation to war:* "Animals in the Bible," NewAdvent.org.

92 *what makes Israel's monarchy unique:* Leslie J. Hoppe, *The Collegeville Bible Commentary*, 215.

93 *the returning waters then engulf the entire Egyptian army:* John F. Craghan, *The Collegeville Bible Commentary*, 95.

94 *The figure on the white horse is said to symbolize Christ:* "Dictionary: Four Horsemen," CatholicCulture.org. Accessed March 04, 2019 at https://www.catholicculture.org/culture/library/dictionary/index.cfm?id=3362.

95 *a local priest still blesses horses:* Mary Rampellini, "Horse Blessing at Oaklawn Tradition for One Trainer," *Arkansas Catholic*, February 15, 2016. Accessed September 17, 2020 at https://www.arkansas-catholic.org/news/article/4576/Horse-blessing-at-Oaklawn-tradition-for-one-trainer.

96 *The animals praise and glorify God:* "Blessing of Horses and Other Draft Animals – Prayers," Catholic.org. Accessed September 17, 2020 at https://www.catholic.org/prayers/prayer.php?p=387

97 *Martin . . . has wrapped Me in his own cloak:* Thomas J. Craughwell, "A Patron Saint for Horseback Riders," CatholicHerald.com. November 8, 2017. Accessed September 17, 2020 at https://www.catholicherald.com/faith/your_faith/the_saints/a_patron_saint_for_horseback_riders

98 *only about 500 purebred Cartujano horses are still in existence:* Rick Yoder, "The Horses of St. Bruno," *The Amish Catholic*, October 6, 2018. Accessed September 17, 2020 at https://amishcatholic.com/2018/10/06/the-horses-of-st-bruno/. And L'Ordre Des Chartreux, "A Calling: St. Bruno," Accessed September 17, 2020 at http://www.chartreux.org/en/origin.php.

99 *noble, docile and well-balanced:* "The Pure Spanish Horse: History," Karapre.com. Accessed September 17, 2020 at https://www.karapre.com/the-pure-spanish-horse.

CHAPTER 11

100 *Dogs in the Bible are represented as filthy, unclean, and loathsome:* "Animals in the Bible," NewAdvent.org.

101 *It may have been an arbitrary test:* John A. Grindel, *The Collegeville Bible Commentary*, 255. And George Leo Haydock, "Commentary on Judges 7:5," George Haydock's Catholic Bible Commentary. Accessed September 17, 2020 at https://www.studylight.org/commentary/judges/7-5.html#hcc.

102 *Lazarus was . . . probably accursed:* Pablo T. Gadenz, *The Gospel of Luke*, 287. And "Animals in the Bible," NewAdvent.org.

103 *characterized by "treachery, ferocity, and bloodthirstiness:* "Animals in the Bible," NewAdvent.org.

104 *the wolves are the people who lead Israel astray:* Daniel J. Harrington, *The Gospel of Matthew*, 108.

105 *the monks would set out with huge dogs:* "Bernard of Montjoux," LoyolaPress.com. Accessed September 17, 2020 at https://www.loyolapress.com/our-catholic-faith/saints/saints-stories-for-all-ages/bernard-of-montjoux.

106 *St. Roch is now forever associated with our canine friends:* "Saint Roch," Roman-Catholic-Saints.com. Accessed September 17, 2020 at https://www.roman-catholic-saints.com/saint-roch.html.

107 *The dog is said to have led her into the forest:* "Saint Margaret of Cortona," FranciscanMedia.org. Accessed September 17, 2020 at https://www.franciscanmedia.org/saint-margaret-of-cortona/.

108 *It sounds ridiculous to call him an angel:* Life Teen, "St. John Bosco: The Saint Who's Praying for You," LifeTeen.com. Accessed September 17, 2020 at https://lifeteen.com/blog/st-john-bosco-the-saint-whos-praying-for-you/.

109 *By developing such strong bonds with your dog:* Marieta Murg, "Why Do Dogs Try to Protect Their Owners – Wag!" WagWalking. Accessed September 17, 2020 at https://wagwalking.com/behavior/why-do-dogs-try-to-protect-their-owners.

110 *The townspeople cared for Brother Wolf:* Taming the Wolf Institute, "Saint Francis & the Wolf." Accessed September 17, 2020 at https://tamingthewolf.com/saint-francis-and-the-wolf/.

CHAPTER 12

111 *the birds . . . have a history in Scripture of pointing our eyes to the holy:* "Birds Are Used as Christian Symbols." Catholicism.org, October 30, 2004. Accessed September 17, 2020 at https://catholicism.org/birds-are-used-as-christian-symbols.html.

112 *It is God who tells Noah to leave the ark:* Pauline Viviano, *The Collegeville Bible Commentary,* 49.

113 *the eagle . . . becomes an actual symbolic representation of God:* Philip Kosloski, "The Fascinating Spiritual Symbolism of the Eagle," Aleteia, August 7, 2017. Accessed September 17, 2020 at https://aleteia.org/2017/08/07/the-fascinating-spiritual-symbolism-of-the-eagle/.

114 *Eagles are capable of sustained flapping flight:* "How Eagles Fly," JourneyNorth.org. Accessed September 17, 2020 at https://journeynorth.org/tm/eagle/EagleFlightLesson.html.

115 *The description of the Spirit's descent:* Daniel J. Harrington, *The Gospel of Matthew,* 62.

116 *the Holy Spirit is so often portrayed as a dove in Christian art:* "Birds Are Used as Christian Symbols." Catholicism.org.

117 *The common house sparrow weighs:* "House Sparrow: Identification," Cornell Lab of Ornithology. Accessed September 17, 2020 at https://www.allaboutbirds.org/guide/House_Sparrow/id.

118 *It would take over one hundred sparrows:* "Bald Eagle: Identification," Cornell Lab of Ornithology. Accessed September 17, 2020 at https://www.allaboutbirds.org/guide/Bald_Eagle/id. And "Mourning Dove: Identification," Cornell Lab of Ornithology. Accessed September 17, 2020 at https://www.allaboutbirds.org/guide/Mourning_Dove/id.

119 *The conclave saw this as a sign of the Holy Spirit's favor:* Charles A. Coulombe, *A History of the Popes: Vicars of Christ.* New York: MJF Books, 2005, 46. And "Pope St. Fabian," Catholic Encyclopedia, NewAdvent.org. Accessed September 17, 2020 at http://www.newadvent.org/cathen/05742d.htm.

120 *This fifteen-hundred-year-old story has everything:* Christopher Klein, "Did an Irish Monk 'Discover' America?" History.com. A&E Television Networks, March 17, 2014. Accessed September 17, 2020 at https://www.history.com/news/did-an-irish-monk-discover-america.

121 *the Work of God (Opus Dei):* USCCB, "Liturgy of the Hours." Accessed September 17, 2020 at http://www.usccb.org/prayer-and-worship/liturgy-of-the-hours/index.cfm.

122 *Brendan visits an island called the Paradise of Birds:* John Joseph O'Meara, *The Voyage of Saint Brendan: Journey to the Promised Land* (Dublin: Dolmen Press, 1978), 19–25.

123 *began to open their beaks, stretch their necks, flap their wings:* Henry Edward Manning, *The Little Flowers of Saint Francis of Assisi,* 49.

124 *take up that loaf, and leave it in some such place:* Abbot Primate Jerome Theisen, OSB, *The Benedictines: An Introduction.* Order of Saint Benedict. Accessed September 17, 2020 at http://www.osb.org/gen/greg/dia-10.html#P72_26907.

125 *Kevin is said to have remained in that position:* Brian Lacey, *O'Brien Pocket History of Irish Saints* (Dublin: O'Brien), 2003, 89.

CHAPTER 13

126 *there are some 10 quintillion . . . individual insects alive:* The Smithsonian, "Numbers of Insects (Species and Individuals)." Accessed September 17, 2020 at https://www.si.edu/spotlight/buginfo/bugnos.

127 *Unlike the first two plagues:* John F. Craghan, *The Collegeville Bible Commentary,* 89.

128 *Livestock and poultry are sometimes killed by the flies:* "The Truth About Buffalo Gnats." College of Agricultural, Consumer and Environmental Sciences, June 18, 2007. Accessed September 17, 2020 at https://aces.illinois.edu/news/truth-about-buffalo-gnats.

129 *In Christianity, [flies] also often represent sin:* Pauly Fongemie, "Signs: Animals," CatholicTradition.org.

130 *grasshoppers . . . can eat up to sixteen times their own body weight:* Pauly Fongemie, "Signs: Animals," CatholicTradition.org. And "Grasshopper – Facts, Diet & Habitat Information," AnimalCorner.org. Accessed September 17, 2020 at https://animalcorner.co.uk/animals/grasshopper/.

131 *render it particularly adapted for bees:* "Animals in the Bible," NewAdvent.org.

132 *the bee has also been a symbol of regal or kingly power:* Pauly Fongemie, "Signs: Animals," CatholicTradition.org.

133 *To preserve her soul and body free from stain:* Davide Bianchini, "Penance & Mortification," ReligiousVocation.com, September 29, 2015. Accessed September 17, 2020 at http://www.religious-vocation.com/penance_and_mortification.html#.XiHgNMhKi1s.

134 *St. Ite of Killedy . . . would let a stag beetle:* "St. Ita of Killeedy," Saint Kateri Tekakwitha Parish, Irondequoit, NY. Accessed March 04, 2019 at http://www.kateriirondequoit.org/resources/saints-alive/ignatius-ivo/st-ita-of-killeedy/.

135 *went to live in a mosquito-infested swamp:* "St. Macarius the Great – Saints & Angels," Catholic.org. Accessed September 17, 2020 at https://www.catholic.org/saints/saint.php?saint_id=4385.

136 *Ambrose is now the patron saint of beekeepers:* St. Ambrose University, "Fighting and Queen Bees." Accessed September 17, 2020 at https://www.sau.edu/about-sau/at-a-glance/history-of-sau/bees. And Franciscan Media, "Saint Ambrose," FranciscanMedia.org. Accessed September 17, 2020 at https://www.franciscanmedia.org/saint-ambrose/.

137 *a swarm of bees landed on her face while she was sleeping in her cradle:* Paul Fongemie, "Mary's Symbols," Accessed September 17, 2020 at http:// http://www.catholictradition.org/Cascia/rita1-2.htm.

138 *a spider quickly spun a web over the door:* "Saint Felix of Nola," CatholicSaints.Info. Accessed September 17, 2020 at https://catholicsaints.info/saint-felix-of-nola/.

ABOUT PARACLETE PRESS

WHO WE ARE

As the publishing arm of the Community of Jesus, Paraclete Press presents a full expression of Christian belief and practice—from Catholic to Evangelical, from Protestant to Orthodox, reflecting the ecumenical charism of the Community and its dedication to sacred music, the fine arts, and the written word. We publish books, recordings, sheet music, and video/DVDs that nourish the vibrant life of the church and its people.

WHAT WE ARE DOING

BOOKS | PARACLETE PRESS BOOKS show the richness and depth of what it means to be Christian. While Benedictine spirituality is at the heart of who we are and all that we do, our books reflect the Christian experience across many cultures, time periods, and houses of worship.

We have many series, including Paraclete Essentials; Paraclete Fiction; Paraclete Poetry; Paraclete Giants; and for children and adults, All God's Creatures, books about animals and faith; and San Damiano Books, focusing on Franciscan spirituality. Others include Voices from the Monastery (men and women monastics writing about living a spiritual life today), Active Prayer, and new for young readers: The Pope's Cat. We also specialize in gift books for children on the occasions of Baptism and First Communion, as well as other important times in a child's life, and books that bring creativity and liveliness to any adult spiritual life.

The MOUNT TABOR BOOKS series focuses on the arts and literature as well as liturgical worship and spirituality; it was created in conjunction with the Mount Tabor Ecumenical Centre for Art and Spirituality in Barga, Italy.

MUSIC | PARACLETE PRESS DISTRIBUTES RECORDINGS of the internationally acclaimed choir Gloriæ Dei Cantores, the Gloriæ Dei Cantores Schola, and the other instrumental artists of the Arts Empowering Life Foundation.

PARACLETE PRESS IS THE EXCLUSIVE NORTH AMERICAN DISTRIBUTOR for the Gregorian chant recordings from St. Peter's Abbey in Solesmes, France. Paraclete also carries all of the Solesmes chant publications for Mass and the Divine Office, as well as their academic research publications.

In addition, PARACLETE PRESS SHEET MUSIC publishes the work of today's finest composers of sacred choral music, annually reviewing over 1,000 works and releasing between 40 and 60 works for both choir and organ.

VIDEO | Our video/DVDs offer spiritual help, healing, and biblical guidance for a broad range of life issues including grief and loss, marriage, forgiveness, facing death, understanding suicide, bullying, addictions, Alzheimer's, and Christian formation.

Learn more about us at our website
www.paracletepress.com
or phone us toll-free at 1-800-451-5006

SCAN
TO
READ